FOCUSING ON THE FUTURE

Key Prophecies
and Practical Living

Jack W. H.

with
Jack Hayford III

THOMAS NELSON PUBLISHERS
Nashville

CONTENTS

Focusing on the Future: Key Prophecies and Practical Living is one of a series of study guides that focus exciting, discovery-geared coverage of Bible book and power themes—all prompting toward dynamic, Holy Spirit-filled living.

About the Executive Editor

JACK W. HAYFORD, noted pastor, teacher, writer, and composer, is the Executive Editor of the complete series, working with the publisher in the conceiving and developing of each of the books.

Dr. Hayford is Senior Pastor of The Church On The Way, the First Foursquare Church of Van Nuys, California. He and his wife, Anna, have four married children, all of whom are active in either pastoral ministry or vital church life. As General Editor of the *Spirit-Filled Life Bible*, Pastor Hayford led a four-year project, which has resulted in the availability of one of today's most practical and popular study Bibles. He is author of more than twenty books, including *A Passion for Fullness, The Beauty of Spiritual Language, Rebuilding the Real You*, and *Prayer Is Invading the Impossible*. His musical compositions number over four hundred songs, including the widely sung "Majesty."

About the Writer

JACK HAYFORD III is a scientific technician, who lives in Neenah, Wisconsin, where he is employed by the Neenah Paper Company, a subsidiary of the Kimberly-Clark Corporation. He is a chemistry graduate (with honors) from Azusa Pacific University in California and did his graduate work at Lawrence University in Appleton, Wisconsin, at the Institute of Paper Science and Technology. He is a member and actively involved in teaching in his local congregation, where he and his wife Joann serve. They have two children: Dawn (7) and Jack IV (5).

Jack's teacher/scientist bent early manifested itself when, as a pastor's son, he taught himself New Testament Greek as a side hobby, along with his interest in chess and wrestling as a member of the Los Angeles High School Championship Team.

His deep interest in Bible and theology made him an able assistant to his father during the editorial preparation of the *Spirit-Filled Life Bible*, released by Thomas Nelson Publishers in 1991.

Of this contributor, the Executive Editor has remarked: "It's a privilege to be involved with Jack in exacting areas of Christian life and thought. His thoroughness of thinking gives his work a quality that will profit every student."

THE KEYS
THAT KEEP ON FREEING

Is there anything that holds more mystery or more genuine practicality than a key? The mystery: "What does it fit? What can it turn on? What might it open? What new discovery could be made? The practicality: Something *will* most certainly open to the possessor! Something *will* absolutely be found to unlock and allow a possibility otherwise obstructed!

- Keys describe the instruments we use to access or ignite.
- Keys describe the concepts that unleash mind-boggling possibilities.
- Keys describe the different structures of musical notes which allow variation and range.

Jesus spoke of keys: "And I will give you the keys of the kingdom of heaven, and whatever you bind on earth will be bound in heaven, and whatever you loose on earth will be loosed in heaven" (Matt. 16:19).

While there is no conclusive list of exactly what keys Jesus was referring to, it is clear that He did confer upon His church—upon *all* who believe—the access to a realm of spiritual partnership with Him in the dominion of His kingdom. Faithful students of the Word of God, moving in the practical grace and biblical wisdom of Holy Spirit-filled living and ministry, have noted some of the primary themes which undergird this order of "spiritual partnership" Christ offers. The "keys" are *concepts*—biblical themes that are traceable through the Scriptures and verifiably dynamic when applied with soundly based faith under the lordship of Jesus Christ. The "partnership" is the *essential* feature of this release of divine grace;

(1) believers reaching to *receive* Christ's promise of "kingdom keys," (2) while choosing to *believe* in the Holy Spirit's readiness to actuate their unleashing, unlimited power today.

Companioned with the Bible book studies in the *Spirit-Filled Life Study Guide* series, the Kingdom Dynamic studies present a dozen different themes. This study series is an outgrowth of the Kingdom Dynamics themes included throughout the *Spirit-Filled Life Bible,* which provide a treasury of insight developed by some of today's most respected Christian leaders. From that beginning, studious writers have evolved the elaborated studies you'll pursue here.

The central goal of the subjects focused on in this present series of study guides is to relate "power points" of the Holy Spirit-filled life. Assisting you in your discoveries are a number of helpful features. Each study guide has twelve to fourteen lessons, each arranged so you can plumb the depths or skim the surface, depending upon your needs and interests. The study guides contain major lesson features, each marked by a symbol and heading for easy identification.

WORD WEALTH

The WORD WEALTH feature provides important definitions of key terms.

BEHIND THE SCENES

BEHIND THE SCENES supplies information about cultural beliefs and practices, doctrinal disputes, business trades, and the like, that illuminate Bible passages and teachings.

AT A GLANCE

The AT A GLANCE feature uses maps and charts to identify places and simplify themes or positions.

 ## KINGDOM EXTRA

Because this study guide focuses on a theme of the Bible, you will find a KINGDOM EXTRA feature that guides you into Bible dictionaries, Bible encyclopedias, and other resources that will enable you to glean more from the Bible's wealth on the topic if you want something extra.

 ## PROBING THE DEPTHS

Another feature, PROBING THE DEPTHS, will explain controversial issues raised by particular lessons and cite Bible passages and other sources to which you can turn to help you come to your own conclusions.

 ## FAITH ALIVE

Finally, each lesson contains a FAITH ALIVE feature. Here the focus is, So what? Given what the Bible says, what does it mean for my life? How can it impact my day-to-day needs, hurts, relationships, concerns, and whatever else is important to me? FAITH ALIVE will help you see and apply the practical relevance of God's literary gift.

As you'll see, these guides supply space for you to answer the study and life-application questions and exercises. You may, however, want to record all your answers, or just the overflow from your study or application, in a separate notebook or journal. This would be especially helpful if you think you'll dig into the KINGDOM EXTRA features. Because the exercises in this feature are optional and can be expanded as far as you want to take them, we have not allowed writing space for them in this study guide. So you may want to have a notebook or journal handy for recording your discoveries while working through to this feature's riches.

The Bible study method used in this series revolves around four basic steps: observation, interpretation, correlation, and application. Observation answers the question, What does the text say? Interpretation deals with, What does the text mean? —not with what it means to you or me, but what it meant to its original readers. Correlation asks, What light do other Scripture passages shed on this text? And application, the goal of Bible study, poses the question, How should my life change in response to the Holy Spirit's teaching of this text?

If you have used a Bible much before, you know that it comes in a variety of translations and paraphrases. Although you can use any of them with profit as you work through the *Spirit-Filled Life Kingdom Dynamics Study Guide* series, when Bible passages or words are cited, you will find they are from the New King James Version of the Bible. Using this translation with this series will make your study easier, but it's certainly not necessary.

The only resources you need to complete and apply these study guides are a heart and mind open to the Holy Spirit, a prayerful attitude, and a pencil and a Bible. Of course, you may draw upon other sources, such as commentaries, dictionaries, encyclopedias, atlases, and concordances, and you'll even find some optional exercises that will guide you into these sources. But these are extras, not necessities. These study guides are comprehensive enough to give you all you need to gain a good, basic understanding of the Bible book being covered and how you can apply its themes and counsel to your life.

A word of warning, though. By itself, Bible study will not transform your life. It will not give you power, peace, joy, comfort, hope, and a number of other gifts God longs for you to unwrap and enjoy. Through Bible study, you will grow in your understanding of the Lord, His kingdom and your place in it, and those things are essential. But you need more. You need to rely on the Holy Spirit to guide your study and your application of the Bible's truths. He, Jesus promised, was sent to teach us "all things" (John 14:26; cf. 1 Cor. 2:13). So as you use this series to guide you through Scripture, bathe your study time in prayer, asking the Spirit of God to illuminate the text, enlighten your mind, humble your will, and comfort your heart. He will never let you down.

My prayer and goal for you is that as you unlock and begin to explore God's Book for living His way, the Holy Spirit will fill every fiber of your being with the joy and power God longs to give all His children. So read on. Be diligent. Stay open and submissive to Him. You will not be disappointed. He promises you!

Lesson 1/The Man and the Message

Prophecy has always been a subject of great interest to Christians. In the early church there were teachers of prophecy ranging from the apostles Paul and John to heretical teachers who caused concern among the Corinthians and Thessalonians (see 1 Cor. 15:12; 2 Thess. 2:1–3). Frequently, speculation has caused concern or excitement. For example, at the time of the Reformation, Martin Luther and others taught that the Roman Catholic establishment was the harlot of Revelation. And the renowned scientist, Sir Isaac Newton, spent years probing the possible meanings of the prophecies of Daniel. Today it is no different; virtually every significant world event is examined and scrutinized by Bible students to determine how it may fit into any one of numerous prophetic schemes.

It is not without reason that this interest is attached to prophetic studies. More than one-fourth of the books of the Bible are prophetic books, and there is much prophetic content in other books as well. Moreover, many of the significant figures in the Bible—Moses, Samuel, David and, of course, Jesus—were prophets. Thus, it is apparent that the office of the prophet and the function of prophecy comprise an important part of God's dealings with mankind.

In beginning a systematic overview of the subject of prophecy, it is appropriate that we look at the men and women who were used in prophetic ministry to discover characteristic elements of prophetic teaching. Let us begin by examining the words and expressions used to designate the prophet himself.

THE TITLES OF THE PROPHET

In the following passages what word is used for God's messenger? Of whom is it used?

2 Kin. 19:1–5

2 Chr. 34:21, 22

Ezra 5:1, 2

 WORD WEALTH

Prophet, *nabi'.* Prophet; one who proclaims or tells a message he has received; a spokesman, herald, announcer. A prophet is someone who announces a message at the direction of another (usually the Lord God). *Nabi'* occurs more than 300 times in the Old Testament. Six times the word is used in the feminine form, *nebiyah,* and it is translated "prophetess"; these six references are to Miriam, Deborah, Huldah (twice), Noadiah, and Isaiah's wife (no doubt a prophetess in her own capacity). In all other references, *nabi'* is masculine, "prophet." The word can refer to false prophets and to prophets of false gods, but nearly always refers to Yahweh's commissioned spokesmen.[1]

Other terms are used less commonly for prophets, but they give insight into other aspects of the prophetic ministry. What other titles are given to prophets in the Bible?

1 Sam. 9:18, 19; 2 Chr. 16:7–10

1 Kin. 13:1–10; 17:17–24

Dan. 9:11; Amos 3:7

 WORD WEALTH

Seer, *ro'eh.* A visionary, a seer; one who sees visions; a prophet. *Ro'eh* comes from the verb *ra'ah,* which means "to see," but also has a wide range of meanings related to seeing (such as "perceive," "appear," "discern," "look," "stare," and many other nuances). It was only natural for Hebrew speakers to describe a prophet as a "seer," since prophets frequently received messages from God through visions. However the word *nabi'* (spokesman) is the preferred Hebrew word for prophet.[2]

THE CALL OF THE PROPHET

Insight into the human response to God's divine appointment of the prophets helps us sense their awakening to His purpose. Let's examine two prophets and their descriptions of their calls. Read Isaiah 6 and Ezekiel 1—3:15.

When these two prophets were called, what did they see? (Is. 6:1; Ezek. 1:1)

How did each respond to his vision?

Is. 6:5

Ezek. 1:28

What was God's command to them?

Is. 6:9

Ezek. 2:7; 3:4

The prophets acted as spokesmen for God. In the following passages, how did God prepare the prophets' mouths (their primary tool) to proclaim His Word?

Is. 6:5–7

Jer. 1:6–10

Ezek. 3:1–3

One title of the prophet was "man of God." The people viewed the prophets as ones who had a special relationship to God. When they were called into this relationship, the prophets frequently gained insight into particular aspects of God's character. What attributes of God are seen in the following verses?

Is. 6:1–3

Jer. 1:5

Ezek. 1:26–28; 3:12

Jon. 4:2

The call of the prophet was an unforgettable, life-changing experience. God was revealed to them in a special way, and they received a message from God for the people. What do the prophets say about the message they were to give?

Jer. 20:9

Amos 3:8

From our study, we see that the prophets were people called into special relationship with God and given a message that they were compelled to proclaim. Let us examine the elements of that message.

THE PREACHING OF THE PROPHET

The message of the prophets was two-pronged: it consisted of proclamation and prediction, or forth-telling (that is, preaching/proclaiming God's Word and will) as well as foretelling (that is, giving notice or warning of God's coming actions or judgments). The Greek word for "prophet" makes this clear.

 WORD WEALTH

Prophet, prophetes. From *pro,* "forth," and *phemi,* "to speak." A prophet, therefore, is primarily a forth-teller, one who speaks forth a divine message that can at times include foretelling future events. Among the Greeks, the prophet was the interpreter of the divine will, and this idea is dominant in biblical usage. Prophets are therefore specially endowed with insights into the counsels of the Lord and serve as His spokesmen. Prophecy is a gift of the Holy Spirit (1 Cor 12:12), which the New Testament encourages believers to exercise, although at a level different from those with the prophetic office (Eph 4:11).[3]

As one who interprets the divine will, the two facets of prophetic preaching—forth-telling and foretelling—come together. Whether in a present call to repentance and holiness, or in the announcement of future events, the final exaltation of God and His will is always paramount. Let us look at some examples. Read Isaiah 2:6–11. List ten reasons for God's forsaking of His people.

1.

2.

3.

4.

5.

6.

7.

8.

9.

10.

Read Jeremiah 7:30–34. For what sins of Judah was judgment declared?

Read Amos 2:4–8 and 2:13–16.

What were the sins of Judah?

What were the sins of Israel?

What judgment is proclaimed against Judah? against Israel?

Read Hosea 10:1–8.

Who was going to break down the altars of Israel? (v. 2)

What was to be the fate of their idol? (vv. 5, 6)

What was to happen to Israel? (vv. 7, 8)

In all of these passages idolatry and a disregard for God's law figure prominently in the sins that were spoken against. Furthermore, although all four passages declare judgment, in

Jeremiah and Hosea we see reference to definite future events. Thus we have the two aspects of prophetic preaching combined in their messages. But beyond this message of repentance from apostasy, prophetic preaching had another concern.

What five things are we told to do in Isaiah 1:17?

1.

2.

3.

4.

5.

What three groups of people in Jeremiah 7:6 are we told not to oppress?

What four groups of people does Zechariah 7:10 exhort us not to oppress?

Name five types of people the Lord will witness against (Mal. 3:5).

The princes of Judah were condemned for four things in Ezekiel 22:6, 7. List them.

We see in these passages another side of prophetic preaching. In addition to calling for obedience, the prophets also called for social justice. Reread Amos 2:6–8. List seven sins mentioned in those three verses.

1.

2.

3.

4.

5.

6.

7.

We see here again the concern for vulnerable and oppressed people mixed with the condemnation of idolatry and immorality. This passage contains several references to ancient lending practices. Amos vehemently spoke out against abuses in these practices, which led to the further enrichment of the wealthy and powerful at the expense of the poor.

 BEHIND THE SCENES

In Amos 2:6–8 there are two particular allusions to ancient lending practices. In verse 8 it refers to "clothes taken in pledge." Clothing, particularly the outer cloak or coat, was regularly given as a pledge for a debt. Under Mosaic Law, when the cloak was given as a pledge, it was to be returned at night (Ex. 22:26; Deut. 24:10–13). Under no circumstances was a widow's garment to be taken in pledge (Deut. 24:17). The second practice referred to was the practice of selling a debtor into slavery in order to pay a debt. In the ancient world a lender could have a man and his family sold into slavery in order to pay a debt (see Matt. 18:21–35). Mosaic Law contained regulations to prevent the abuse of this practice (Deut. 15:12–18), but it was a lawful practice.

THE PRAYING OF THE PROPHET

Though they proclaimed judgment from God, the prophets were men who cared deeply about their nation's citizens. Another function of the prophet was to be an intercessor.

Read 1 Samuel 12:23; 1 Kings 18:41–46; Jeremiah 7:12–16; Daniel 9:1–3; and Amos 7:1–6.

Who were the prophets who were shown to be intercessors?

Who was commanded to stop interceding?

Why was the prophet commanded not to pray?

THE PROOF OF THE PROPHET

The true prophet of God frequently had an unpopular message. And there were always false prophets who were willing to tell the people what they wanted to hear. How could the people of God distinguish between the true and false prophets?

According to Deuteronomy 18:20–22 how can one tell if a prophet is not from God?

It is important to note carefully the wording in the above passage. If a word spoken does not come to pass, he who spoke is a false prophet. However, if the word does come to pass, we are not to automatically conclude that the prophet was sent by God.

Read Deuteronomy 13:1–5. If a sign given by a prophet comes to pass, on what basis can one still determine that the prophet is not from God?

We see again that obedience to God is the final determinant of true prophecy. A true prophet of God would never contradict God's Law given through Moses. It was this belief that led the Pharisees to oppose Jesus so vehemently. They saw Jesus as a lawbreaker and, therefore, as a false prophet. They could not see that it was their own interpretation of the Law that was in error, and that, in fact, Jesus was the long-awaited Prophet, whose coming Moses had foretold (Deut. 18:15).

MOSES—THE PARADIGM OF A PROPHET

Moses was seen as the model prophet from early in Hebrew history. The prophets were measured against his example, and orthodoxy was measured against his teaching. In the following chart we see characteristics of prophetic ministry which we have examined, and examples of their manifestation in Moses' ministry.

AT A GLANCE

FACET OF PROPHETIC MINISTRY	ILLUSTRATED IN MOSES' MINISTRY
Called by God	Ex. 3:1—4:17
Called for obedience	Deut. 4:1–40
Called for social justice	Num. 27:1–11
Interceded for the people	Ex. 32:7–14
Foretold future events	Deut. 18:15–19

FAITH ALIVE

How has your view of prophetic ministry in the Bible been enlarged?

Seeing that the biblical yardstick for judging prophets was adherence to the Scripture, how should we examine the teaching we receive?

Let us thank God for His Word, and ask Him to "guide us into all truth" (John 16:13) by His Spirit.

1. *Spirit-Filled Life Bible* (Nashville, TN: Thomas Nelson Publishers, 1991), 401, "Word Wealth: 3:20 prophet."
2. Ibid., 407, "Word Wealth: 9:9 seer."
3. Ibid., 1405, "Word Wealth: 2:5 prophet."

Lesson 2/Characteristics of Prophecy

In examining the ministry of the prophets, we have seen that they were primarily spokesmen for God. They were men who called for righteousness: righteousness (right behavior) in relationship to God and righteousness (just practice) in relationship to one's neighbor. This was the crux of the prophetic message.

However, we cannot forget the role of foretelling in prophetic preaching, for the prophets were not just religious or social reformers. They were men and women who claimed God's authority in their message and whose message was confirmed—in part by correct proclamation of future events. This aspect of the prophetic ministry is so prominent that "prophecy" has come to be synonymous with "foretelling."

As we consider the predictive aspect of prophetic literature, what are the key concepts which enable us to interpret prophecy? Why did the prophets prophesy?

PROPHECY IS DISCURSIVE

In interpreting and understanding the prophetic scriptures it is important to realize that prophecy is discursive. "Discursive" basically means that the speaker or writer often moves from one subject to another with no reference to time, timing, or a particular order. As this term applies to prophecy it refers to the fact that the prophets saw visions and reported what they saw. However, their visions did not necessarily relate to one another in any sequential, chronological, or orderly way. Two prophecies in sequence may end up being fulfilled chronologically, in reversed order, or they may not be directly connected to each other at all. In other cases, the prophet would not be aware of large gaps of time within his own prophecy. In much the same way an observer may look at a range of mountains but not be able to specify the size of the valleys between sets of peaks within the total range, the time between prophecies would elude the prophet.

Again, a prophet may have visions that overlap, as though he were seeing the same event from a series of different perspectives. The discursive nature of prophecy is one of the most basic things to realize about prophecy in the Bible.

Read Micah 4 and 5. Note the following division of sections in these two chapters:

Section 1: 4:1–5

Section 2: 4:6–8

Section 3: 4:9, 10

Section 4: 4:11–13

Section 5: 5:1

Section 6: 5:2–5a

Section 7: 5:5b, 6

Section 8: 5:7–9

Section 9: 5:10–15

When will Section 1 be fulfilled?

How does Section 2 compare to Section 1 chronologically?

To what event does Section 3 refer?

In Section 4 what role does the "daughter of Zion" hold with respect to the nations?

In Section 5 is Judah victorious or being oppressed?

To whom does Section 6 refer?

Compare Micah 5:3 with 4:10.

In Section 7, who delivers Judah from the Assyrians? (Note the context in Section 6.)

In Section 8 is Israel victorious or being oppressed?

What action is the Lord taking in Section 9?

To whom is the Lord speaking in Section 9?

Compare Section 4 and Section 8.

Micah 4:6 and 5:10 both use the phrase "in that day." Are they referring to the same time? Explain.

Which of the sections possibly overlap?

How would you put the sections in chronological order?

The above investigation should help one understand the discursive nature of prophecy. Micah jumps back and forth from the latter days to future Babylonian captivity to their contemporary struggle with Assyria to the coming of the Messiah to Jacob's being victorious among the nations and the Lord's cleansing His people and judging the wicked. All of that is covered in just 28 verses!

Let us look at some additional examples of discursive elements in prophecy.

EXAMPLE OF NON-SEQUENTIAL PROPHECY

Read Isaiah 9.

When was Isaiah 9:1, 2 fulfilled?

When was Isaiah 9:6 fulfilled?

Is Isaiah 9:7 already fulfilled, yet to be fulfilled, or ongoing in its fulfillment?

What do verses 8–21 refer to? Has this been fulfilled? When?

What does the sequence of these prophecies in chapter 9 show us about the discursive nature of prophecy?

EXAMPLE OF OVERLAPPING OF PROPHECY

The clearest example of the overlapping of prophetic visions is found in Daniel, but first some historical background on some of the events related to this book.

 BEHIND THE SCENES

In 539 B.C. Cyrus overthrew Babylon and established the suzerainty of Persia over the old Babylonian Empire. Persia was the dominant power throughout the Middle East for more than 200 years. But later, in 334 B.C., Alexander the Great crossed the Granicus River and began his conquest of the Persian Empire. Alexander moved with incredible swiftness, and within ten years of his original foray into Asia Minor, he had conquered all the kingdoms from Asia Minor to Egypt and from Tyre to the border of India.

However, Alexander the Great died in 323 B.C., and fighting broke out among his generals. For twenty-two years a power struggle raged over the loosely connected empire. Finally, in 301 B.C. a decisive battle was fought after which the victors divided Alexander's empire into four parts: Seleucus ruled over Syria, Lysimachus ruled Thrace, Cassander took the kingdom of Macedonia, and Ptolemy became the ruler of Egypt.

With that information in mind, read Daniel 7 and 8 and 11:2–4.

When did Daniel receive these visions?

What two kingdoms are common to the three visions?

In Daniel 8:5 and 8:8 who is represented by the large horn of the male goat?

In Daniel 11:3 who is the "mighty king"?

What historic fact is represented by the four heads of the leopard in Daniel 7:6, the four horns in 8:8, and the division of the kingdom "toward the four winds of heaven" in 11:4?

What other parallels do you see in these visions?

From this investigation it is abundantly clear that in three separate visions Daniel was seeing the same historic events. Nowhere else in prophetic literature is the overlapping of different visions so obvious, but this instance should teach us. We can see this overlap from the vantage point of hindsight. But it may be that some prophecies yet future (for example, in Revelation) may eventually prove to overlap more than we realize now.

EXAMPLES OF TIME GAPS WITHIN PROPHECY

Time gaps are very common phenomena in prophetic

writing, for the prophets frequently saw and reported significant events without being aware of their separation in time.

Read Joel 2:28–32.

When was this prophecy fulfilled?

Was the entire prophecy fulfilled?

Where is the break between the portion that has come to pass and the portion that is yet to be fulfilled?

In Joel's original prophecy is there any indication of this time gap?

We see in this example a time gap that, thus far, has been over 1,900 years. Joel apparently had no idea that the gap existed. He saw the last days coming with an outpouring of the Spirit and with God's judgment.

Another example of a time gap in prophecy is in Ezekiel's prophecy of the destruction of Tyre. Let us examine the history of that event and then see how it relates to Ezekiel's prophecy.

 BEHIND THE SCENES

Tyre was a great trade center in Phoenicia at the time of Nebuchadnezzar. The city was built in two parts: one section of the city was on the mainland, and a second part was built on an island about 1/2 mile offshore. In 585 B.C. Nebuchadnezzar laid siege to Tyre, a siege that lasted thirteen years. The end result is unclear, but it is probable that Nebuchadnezzar destroyed the mainland portion of the city. Most of the people and the wealth of Tyre escaped to the island city. Nebuchadnezzar may have received a token surrender in 572 B.C.

In 332 B.C. Alexander the Great attacked Tyre. He was determined to subdue Tyre, for he could not afford to have a strong, unconquered city threatening from the rear when he went on to Egypt and Babylon. During a seven-month siege he built a mole, or causeway, across the channel between the mainland and the island. Although hampered by Tyrian naval attacks on the mole, he succeeded in spanning the channel by literally scraping the rubble off the site of the city that Nebuchadnezzar had destroyed. Then, with a combination of naval and land forces, he managed to breach the defenses of the city and destroy it.

In the light of these historic facts, read Ezekiel's forecast years earlier (Ezek. 26:7–14 and 29:17–20). Now answer the following:

Who would come against Tyre according to Ezekiel's prophecy?

What pronoun is used for the attacker in 26:8–11?

What pronoun is used for the attacker in verse 12?

What does Ezekiel 29:17–20 say about Nebuchadnezzar's success against Tyre?

How did this come to pass historically?

In view of the historical background, who is referred to by "they" in Ezekiel 26:12?

How much time passed between the fulfillment of Ezekiel 26:7–11 and 26:12–14?

Multiple Fulfillment of Prophecy

Having seen examples of the various aspects of the discursive nature of prophecy, we turn to another characteristic of prophecy that is important to understand in order to interpret prophecy. Frequently, a message given by a prophet will have more than one fulfillment: a proximate, or more immediate, short-term fulfillment, as well as a more distant (in time) fulfillment. This is important to keep in mind in studying prophecy. It is quite possible that more than one application of a biblical prophecy is correct, for the prophet's vision could see a fact, but not necessarily know or see how, from different aspects, the same prophecy would be fulfilled in its own way at different times.

Perhaps the most well-known example of multiple fulfillment is the Immanuel prophecy in Isaiah 7.

Read Isaiah 7:1–17 and 8:1–10.

Who was the ultimate fulfillment of this prophecy? (Compare Matt. 1:18–25.)

Consider Isaiah 7:16. Was there another more immediate or proximate fulfillment of this prophecy?

Compare Isaiah 7:16 and 8:4; also consider the use of the name "Immanuel" in 8:8 and the phrase "God *is* with us" in 8:10. Who was the child who initially fulfilled the prophecy of Isaiah 7:14?

PROBING THE DEPTHS

In 1952 the Revised Standard Version was published and caused no small stir in its treatment of Isaiah 7:14. Because they translated the Hebrew word *almah* as "young woman" rather than giving the traditional Authorized Version reading of "virgin," the translators were accused of denying the virgin birth. The fact of the matter is that the word *almah* can mean either "young woman" or "virgin." Earlier translators, recognizing the messianic fulfillment of this prophecy, had translated *almah* as "virgin." The translators of the Revised Standard Version saw that this prophecy was fulfilled in Isaiah 8 as well as in the birth of Jesus. With that in view, they chose the translation "young woman." Some may still extend the controversy, but it is unnecessary. The New Testament gives clear witness to the truth of the virgin birth. The Greek word *parthenos,* which indisputably means "virgin," is used in speaking of the birth of Christ (Luke 1:27) even though the dual application of the Isaiah 7:14 passage required the use of a less precise, but no less pure, term.

Read Micah 7:1–7 and Matthew 10:34–39.

What is Micah speaking of directly in 7:1–7?

To what does Jesus apply verse 6 from Micah's prophecy?

Read Isaiah 6:8–13 and Matthew 13:10–17. How do these passages illustrate a multiple fulfillment of prophecy?

THE PURPOSE OF PROPHECY

We have seen that prophecy can be nonsequential, contain time gaps, and exhibit overlap and multiple fulfillment. These characteristics can make prophecy difficult to understand. Indeed, the prophets themselves did not understand all of what they saw. What does 1 Peter 1:10–12 say in this regard?

The fact that prophets then and students now often do not understand the precise application of some prophecy should not trouble us. God's purposes in giving prophecy are greater than merely satisfying man's curiosity about the future. Rather, God spoke through the prophets in order to demonstrate His foreknowledge and to show His control of human events.

Read Isaiah 41:21–29.

In this passage God is speaking, as it were, to idols. What three types of proof does He demand from them to show that they are gods?

Which type of proof is repeatedly mentioned?

Here Isaiah explicitly denounces the idols as gods. Their main fault? They have no knowledge of things to come. In contrast to that, the Lord tells of the coming of His Servant in subsequent chapters. Look at the following passages and discover who the Servant of the Lord is.

Is. 42:1–4

Is. 44:28—45:7

This entire portion of Isaiah is actually an example of multiple fulfillment of prophecy. Many portions are messianic, yet they also refer to Cyrus of Persia who would allow the Jews to return to their land and rebuild the temple. But in addition, Isaiah is showing that the Lord proves He is God by announcing beforehand what is going to happen, a thing that the idols (that is, the demon-gods) cannot do.

Read Daniel 2:20–23. What does this passage show about God's foreknowledge and control of earthly events?

In addition to demonstrating God's foreknowledge and control, prophecy is given as a means to confirm the prophet's message.

Read Deuteronomy 18:20–22.

What was an indication that a prophet was not from the Lord?

What was the penalty for speaking false prophecy?

So we see that there was great incentive for the prophet to have confirmation of what he spoke. Read Isaiah 44:24–26. Comment on how the Lord works in relation to false prophets ("babblers," "diviners") as opposed to the true prophets, His servants.

Read the following texts and note another purpose for prophecy.

Ezek. 14:21–23

Zech. 1:17

Rom. 15:4

1 Thess. 4:16–18

The comfort of the prophetic message is the most precious and most tender of God's purposes in giving prophecy. He wishes to reveal His foreknowledge and control, and He confirms the prophetic preaching which calls for repentance. But He is also a gracious and loving Father, who cares for His own.

 FAITH ALIVE

What have you learned that is new to you?

How do God's purposes in prophecy relate to you and impact your life?

How does seeing God's confirmation of His Word in past events affect your confidence in His ability to carry out His promises?

What promise has God given you that you can now grasp with greater faith and confidence?

Lesson 3/ Major Themes and Concepts in Prophecy

Having examined the ministry and message of the prophets, and having seen some of the features that aid our understanding of prophetic literature, we are now prepared to look at four key ideas that will help us integrate the message of prophecy throughout the Bible. The concepts we will look at do not begin to exhaust the parallels and common elements one can find in the prophetic writings. But they are very significant themes found throughout the Old and New Testaments, and they help us tie together and mesh the views of the prophets and writers in both Testaments.

THE DAY OF THE LORD

The "day of the LORD" is a key idea in much of the prophetic writings. It is mentioned repeatedly by most of the prophets.

Read Isaiah 13:6–10 and Ezekiel 30:1–4.

What "day" do these scriptures refer to?

What is the common vocal response called for by both Isaiah and Ezekiel?

What common characteristics of that day do both prophets mention?

WORD WEALTH

Day, *yom.* Day; daylight; a day consisting of nighttime and daytime; also, a certain period of time. *Yom* occurs more than 2,200 times with a variety of meanings. *Yom* occurs first in Gen. 1:5, where God called the light "Day"; the remainder of the verse shows that day is not only the period of light, but also a period consisting of evening and morning. (Because God placed evening before morning throughout the week of creation, the Jewish day begins at sundown.) *Yom* may represent a time period or the occasion of a major event. "Day of trouble" (Zeph. 1:15) is thus a troubled time. In Genesis 3:5 and Isaiah 12:4, *yom* expresses an indefinite future time. *Yom Yahweh* ("day of the LORD") may refer to a time when God reveals Himself through judgment and supernatural events. "The day of the LORD" may also refer to the return of the Lord Jesus to judge and rule the world.[1]

Look at the following scriptures and note what the prophets say about the Day of the Lord.

Joel 2:1, 2

Amos 5:18–20

Obad. 15

Zeph. 1:7–9

1 Thess. 5:1–3

2 Pet. 3:10–12

In other references, alternate expressions are used for the "day of the LORD." Examine the following texts and list the expressions that are used for the "day of the LORD."

Is. 63:3–6

Hosea 9:5–7

Joel 2:31

Zeph. 2:1–3

Zeph. 3:8

Mal. 4:1

2 Thess. 1:9, 10; 2:3

Rev. 6:15–17

In all of the above texts we see the prophets speaking of a coming day of judgment: this is the "day of the LORD." It is a day wherein God directly intervenes in human history and brings judgment to the world. But there is another side of the "day of the LORD." Look at the following verses and note what is proclaimed besides judgment.

Joel 3:14–21

Amos 9:8–12

Zeph. 3:8–13

Mal. 4:1–3

2 Thess. 1:9, 10

2 Pet. 3:10–13

So the Day of the Lord contains not only judgment, but salvation and comfort for the righteous as well. The prophets recognized that the Lord would irrupt into history, and that this event would have profound consequences for both the wicked and the righteous. However, the prophetic vision frequently could not differentiate between proximate and more distant events. They sometimes did not see great gaps in time, as we learned in our previous lesson. Thus they saw both impending judgment and other future events as manifestations of the Day of the Lord.

 PROBING THE DEPTHS

The "day of the LORD" is a term used by the Old Testament prophets to signify a time in the history of mankind when God directly intervenes to bring salvation to His people and punishment to the rebellious. By it God restores His righteous order in the Earth. The terms "that Day" and simply "the

Day" are sometimes used as synonyms for the fuller expression "the day of the LORD."

The fulfillment of the Day may be seen in four different ways: 1) In the times of the prophets it was revealed by such events as the invasion of Israel by foreign powers (Amos), the awesome plagues of locusts (Joel), and the return of Israelite exiles from captivity (Ezra-Neh.). 2) In that prophetic insight had the quality of merging periods of eschatology so that even the prophets themselves could not always distinguish the various times of the fulfillment of their prophecies, that Day developed into a broad biblical concept. Prophetic fulfillments closest to the prophets' own day were mingled with those reaching as far as the final culmination of all things. Hence, the First Coming of Christ and the church age began another phase of the Day of the Lord. As participants in this aspect of the Day, the living church—believers like us—can call on the risen Christ to cast down forces that hinder God's work in this present world and to bring about innumerable blessings. This is clear in comparing Isaiah 61:1, 2 with Luke 4:18, 19 and Joel 2:28–32 with Acts 2:16–21. 3) The Second Coming of Christ will inaugurate the third aspect of the Day of the Lord, during which Christ's righteousness and universal rule will restore God's order to the Earth (Amos 9:13; Is. 11:6–9). 4) The ultimate fulfillment of the Day of the Lord awaits the full arrival of the world to come, with its new heaven and new earth. Compare Ezekiel 47:1–12 with Revelation 22:1–5.[2]

JUDGMENT IN ANCIENT HEBREW THOUGHT

A second concept that will enable us to correlate different prophecies is the Hebrew concept of judgment. Generally, when we think of judgment, particularly the judgment of God, we think of wrath or punishment. This was not entirely true of ancient Hebrew thought. To the Hebrews judgment always contained two sides: there was the aspect of punishment that was visited upon the wicked, but equally present in the idea was the deliverance of the righteous. This concept may be more easily understood if we liken it to a civil suit in one of our courts.

In a civil case a decision will be handed down; that is the judgment. Contained in the judgment are two things—the injured party receives recompense for the injury he has received. The guilty party is penalized—they are required to pay the compensation. Thus we see that the Hebrew concept is not really that foreign to our own experience.

WORD WEALTH

Judge, *shaphat.* One who judges, governs, passes down judgment, pronounces sentence, and decides matters. The root is *shaphat,* to "judge," "decide," and "pronounce sentence." In English both "to judge" and "judgment" have negative associations, but not so in Hebrew. Judgment is the balance, ethics, and wisdom, which, if present in a ruler's mind, enables him to govern equitably and to keep the land free from injustice. Judgment, when used of God, is that divine faculty whereby He runs the universe righteously, handing down decisions that will maintain or bring about a right state of affairs. Abraham described God as the Judge of the whole Earth (Gen. 18:25). In the Book of Judges, God raised up human judges *(shophtim)* who governed Israel, executed justice, and handed down decisions.[3]

In viewing the Day of the Lord we have already seen illustration of this idea of judgment in the dual nature of that Day. Let us see some additional illustrations of this concept.

Read Psalm 52.

List five sins of the "mighty man" in verses 1–4.

What is the pivotal verse in this Psalm?

What will be the judgment against the wicked?

What is the response of the righteous?

What is the reward of the righteous?

In the following verses, note the salvation of the righteous versus the end of the wicked. How is it described?

Prov. 2:21, 22

Is. 11:4

Jer. 30:18–24

Hab. 3:12, 13

Matt. 13:41–43

2 Thess. 1:5–7

THIS AGE AND THE AGE TO COME

Another concept that is closely related to, and flows out of, the Jewish understanding of the Day of the Lord and Old Testament prophecy is the idea of time being divided into two segments: this age and the age to come. This idea flows naturally out of the doctrine of the Day of the Lord. The prophets taught that the Lord would break into human affairs at the "day of the LORD" and He would set up His kingdom. After that the Lord would rule "with a rod of iron"—by His absolute power He would rule all the nations. His rule would be in absolute righteousness; therefore, the age to come would be a time of righteousness. In contrast to that, "this present evil age" (Gal. 1:4) is dominated by wickedness and rebellion against God. This view of history was common in the first century A.D. and was shared by the early Christians and Jews.[4] Let us examine some passages which show this view.

Read Luke 20:34–36.

Who is speaking in this text?

Those who attain "that age" also attain what? (v. 35)

What does verse 36 tell us about those who attain "that age"?

Keep in mind that the things spoken of "that age" are spoken of in contrast to what is true of "this age."

Read Matthew 12:31, 32.

Can this sin against the Holy Spirit (essentially, to reject His testimony of Jesus as Son and Savior) ever be forgiven?

What does this imply about the duration of "the *age* to come"?

These texts show that Jesus used this point of view in His teaching. We now turn to the epistles to see this idea in the apostolic writings.

Read 1 Corinthians 2:6–8.

Who are the "rulers of this age"? (Compare Eph. 2:1, 2 and 6:12.)

What is the end of those rulers? (v. 6)

When did God ordain the mystery of redemption? (v. 7)

Why is "ages" plural in verse 7?

Read 1 Corinthians 10:1–13.

What five things were true of "all our fathers" in verses 1–4?

What five things are we warned against by their example? (vv. 6–10)

Why were "these things" written? (v. 11)

For whom were these things written? (v. 11)

Read Galatians 1:4. How does Paul describe the present times?

Read Ephesians 1:20, 21.

Where is Christ seated?

Note the end of verse 21. What does this tell us about Christ's position?

Read Ephesians 2:4–7.

Where are we seated in Christ? (Compare previous reference.)

When will God reveal the full riches of the grace He has given us?

Read Hebrews 9:24–26.

When did Christ appear to present the sacrifice of Himself?

Compare this reference with 1 Corinthians 10:1–13 above. According to both writers, what period were they living in?

Word Wealth

Age, *aion.* Denotes an indefinitely long period, with emphasis on the characteristics of the period rather than its duration. In idiomatic usage it designates "forever" or "forever and ever" (Matt. 21:19; Rom. 16:27; Eph. 3:21). The word is also used as a designation for the present age (Matt. 12:32; 13:22; 1 Tim. 6:17) and for the time after Christ's Second Coming (Mark 10:30; Luke 20:35).[5]

The Kingdom of God

Our final theme for this lesson will be the "kingdom of God." This familiar phrase is so abundantly present, especially in the New Testament, yet the meaning is often misapplied or misunderstood. It can be confusing for two reasons: 1) the terminology is used in various ways in Scripture, and 2) as we saw in the word "judgment," many people have a characteristic way of thinking about "kingdom" that is not in line with the Bible's use of that term.

Many people tend to think of a place when they think of a kingdom. Therefore, when some think of the kingdom of God, they think of heaven. Now heaven is undeniably one expression of the kingdom of God, but Jesus also said, "the kingdom of God is within you" (Luke 17:21). So is the kingdom merely an expression for salvation? No, for Jesus also said that His miracles (specifically the casting out of demons) were a sign that "the kingdom of God has come upon you" (Matt. 12:28).

To discover what the Bible is talking about when it refers to "kingdom," we need to understand the meaning of the Hebrew and Greek words.

> The *primary* meaning of both the Hebrew word *malkuth* in the Old Testament and of the Greek word *basileia* in the New Testament is the rank, authority and sovereignty exercised by a king. A *basileia* may indeed be a realm over which a sovereign exercises his authority; and it may be the people who belong to that realm and over whom authority is exercised; but these are secondary and derived meanings. First of all, a kingdom is the authority to rule, the sovereignty of the king.[6]

Thus the idea behind "kingdom of God" is "the authority of God's rule." This rulership of God is manifest as both a present reality and a future potentiality. Let us see how this helps us understand references to the kingdom.

Read Matthew 16:28—17:8.

Given the context of Jesus' remarks in 16:28, who did "not taste death" before seeing a manifestation of Jesus in His kingdom?

What was the manifestation of the kingdom they witnessed?

How does understanding the meaning of "kingdom" as "the authority or sovereignty of the king" help us to better understand Jesus' saying?

Read Luke 13:18–21.

In the first parable to what does Jesus liken the kingdom of God?

In the second parable what represents the kingdom of God?

If we understood "kingdom" geographically, how would we be forced to interpret these parables?

Understanding the kingdom as Christ's ruling authority, what do you understand these parables to say?

PROBING THE DEPTHS

The Parables of the Mustard Seed and the Leaven. These two parables have been the source of two radically different interpretations. One interpretation sees the birds in the first parable and the leaven in the second parable as representing sin or Satan. According to this interpretation of the mustard seed parable, the kingdom of God grows and matures, but then Satan comes in and finds a place to dwell within the church (kingdom of God). This view interprets the leaven in the second parable as sin that gets into the church (kingdom of God) and works its way throughout it.

The other interpretation, which seems more supportable, sees these parables as statements of the unstoppable growth of God's authority wherever it is received. The mustard seed parable shows the kingdom of God becoming a tree large enough to be a shelter for those who would dwell within it. In the second parable leaven represents the kingdom of God, not sin. (Jesus Himself says, "It [the kingdom of God] is like leaven. . . .") Just as the leaven will work its way through the whole lump of dough, God's ruling authority will continue its work to completion. His promise to complete His work applies to us personally (Phil. 1:6) and to the world as a whole (Rev. 11:15).

Read Matthew 6:31–33.

What three things do the Gentiles seek after?

What two things are we to seek?

Does understanding the "kingdom of God" as "God's authority to rule" change your perspective on this passage? How?

Since Jesus came to begin to open up the "kingdom of God," that is, the possibility of God's rule within us and within our sphere of influence, we can experience His resources for us, for our marriages, for our families, for our jobs, and for every area of our lives. But we must learn to seek His rulership, which means we submit to His ways: "Your kingdom come. Your will be done."

Read Hebrews 1:8. What words are used to signify the rulership or authority of the Son?

Read 1 Corinthians 4:20. How does understanding the kingdom of God in terms of rulership and authority help clarify this verse?

These four themes we have studied are entwined throughout prophecy. The *Day of the Lord* is seen as His irruption into history to bring *judgment*. This judgment has the dual aspects of punishment of the wicked and deliverance for the righteous. That Day brings "this present evil age" to a close and ushers in the *age to come* when the *kingdom of God* is established on earth. At the present time we see that some aspects of the Day of the Lord have already been fulfilled, and God's kingdom authority is already active in His church. But we look forward to that Day when Christ returns to finalize the work of redeeming the world, which He has begun. Seeing that the Day is near, "what manner *of persons* ought you to be in holy conduct and godliness"? (2 Pet. 3:11). How would you answer that inquiry?

1. *Spirit-Filled Life Bible* (Nashville, TN: Thomas Nelson Publishers, 1991), 1350, "Word Wealth: 1:7 day."

2. Ibid., 1306, "Kingdom Dynamics: The 'Day of the Lord' in Prophecy."

3. Ibid., 349, "Word Wealth: 2:18 judge."

4. Ladd, George Eldon, *The Gospel of the Kingdom* (Grand Rapids, MI: Wm. B. Eerdmans Publishing Co., 1959), 28.

5. *Spirit-Filled Life Bible*, 1464, "Word Wealth: 28:20 age."

6. Ladd, 19.

Lesson 4/Messianic Prophecy, Part 1: Pictures or Types of Christ in the Old Testament

No study of biblical prophecy would be complete without considering messianic prophecy. The heart of the message of the Bible is redemption, and the central figure in redemptive history is the Messiah, Jesus Christ. Furthermore, He is the central figure in prophecy—not only in the fact that He is the one spoken of in prophecy, but also in that the very spirit, or life-breath, of prophecy consistently testifies to Him. Verify this by writing out Revelation 19:10.

In this chapter we will look at types, or symbols, of Jesus in the Old Testament. Although not explicit prophecies, these types showed many aspects of the person and work of the Messiah; some of them were even recognized as being messianic in that day.

A *type* is a person, object, place, or event that represents or provides an example of another. "Types" of Christ in the Old Testament show us pictures of Him and His work of deliverance. Their purpose is to further instruct us in the plan of God and the scope of redemption. Furthermore, as with all prophecy, they demonstrate God's foreknowledge and providential control of human events.

Before we look at some messianic types in the Old Testament, let us examine a biblical use of Old Testament types.

Read Galatians 4:21–31.

What are symbols of the two covenants?

What other symbols does Paul use for the Old Covenant?

Paul draws an analogy between the status of the two mothers and the covenants they represent. Explain this analogy.

How does Paul see the relationship of the sons corresponding to his present-day situation? (v. 29)

What does this analogy show you about our position under the new covenant? (v. 31)

We see that the writers of the New Testament saw the importance of Old Testament types. The Book of Hebrews makes extensive use of types, and Paul tells us that the events of Old Testament history occurred so as to be examples to us (1 Cor. 10:11). Jesus Himself, referring to the scriptures of the Old Testament, made clear that they spoke of Him both directly and in type. What did He say the Scriptures do, and what verb describes what we should thereby do? (John 5:39)

How did Jesus Himself support this directive in Luke 24:27?

Thus, we have good precedence for recognizing and studying types in the Old Testament.

TYPES IN THE PENTATEUCH

Read Numbers 21:4–9 and John 3:14, 15.

What represents Jesus in this Old Testament passage?

What does a serpent usually represent?

How does 2 Corinthians 5:21 help us reconcile these apparently conflicting figures?

What did the people need to do in order not to die from the sting of the fiery serpents?

What did Jesus say people would need to do in order not to die from the sting of sin?

This type illustrates beautifully what a type is supposed to do: give a prophetic illustration of an aspect of God's redemptive plan. The history of the bronze serpent also provides a poignant example of how easily man can end up focusing on the instrument of God's blessing instead of worshiping the God who provided the blessing. In 2 Kings we are told that the children of Israel ended up worshiping the bronze serpent (2 Kin. 18:4). Even God's blessing can become a stumbling block if you don't remain focused on Him.

Read Exodus 12:1–14.

What is the topic of this text?

What symbolizes Jesus in this text? (cf. John 1:29; 1 Cor. 5:7)

Against whom was the Lord executing judgment? (v. 12)

What sign protected the Israelites? (v. 13) What was the significance of that sign?

What is the significance of the lamb being without blemish? (v. 5)

In the institution of the Passover we see another picture of our deliverance through the work of Christ. We can also learn another valuable thing about types: do not attempt to make every detail of the type significant. Types give us an illustration to instruct us in the Lord's purposes; however, they were also actual historic events or people. As such, they had a purpose for existing that is separate from being a symbol of God's redemptive work. In our short examination we have in no way exhausted the symbolic material in the Passover. But we must keep in mind that the immediate purpose of the Passover was to remind Israel of their deliverance from Egypt; it is also a picture (or type) of our deliverance from bondage to sin.

TYPES IN THE RELIGIOUS SYSTEM OF MOSES

In the tabernacle and sacrificial system there are many symbols of Christ and His work. Entire books have been written dealing only with the study of those types. We will look at just a couple of types from the Mosaic system of worship, but first let us take a closer look at the tabernacle itself.

 BEHIND THE SCENES

"How lovely *is* Your Tabernacle, O LORD of hosts!" wrote the psalmist. "My soul longs, yes, even faints for the courts of the LORD" (Ps. 84:1, 2). This adoration and devotion was given to the tabernacle because, as the temple was later, it was the focal point of the worship of Yahweh, and it was the primary manifestation of the presence of the Lord among the people of Israel.

Moses was told to build the tabernacle and was given the pattern while he was on Mount Sinai receiving the Law. The mobile structure was ideally suited for a wandering people; but more importantly, it was designed to be an object lesson of God's covenant.

The tabernacle itself was a tent, which was divided into two parts. The innermost chamber of the tabernacle was called the Most Holy Place, and it contained the Ark of the Covenant, which represented the presence of God. Passing through a heavy veil from the Most Holy Place, one would come out to the holy place. The holy place housed the altar of incense directly before the veil, and the table of showbread and the golden lampstand of the left and right respectively. Exiting the tabernacle one came out into a court which was about 50 yards long and 25 yards wide. It was here that the people would bring their sacrifices. The bronze-covered altar lay just beyond the bronze laver as one came out of the tabernacle. Upon this altar the sacrifice would be burned after the blood had been sprinkled around the altar.

Each of these items and their arrangement had its own significance, for the tabernacle was built according to God's pattern (see Ex. 25:9, 40).

Read Exodus 26:31–35.

What object in the tabernacle does this text mainly describe?

What parts of the tabernacle did the veil divide from one another?

What piece of furniture was within the veil?

What did the Ark of the Covenant represent?

According to Hebrews 9:6–8, what does the veil illustrate?

What happened to the veil when Jesus died? (See Matt. 27:51; Mark 15:38; Luke 23:45.)

What does Hebrews 10:19–22 tell us about our current access into the Holiest?

What does the above example of the veil tell us about Jesus' work in the redemptive plan of God?

In addition to the tabernacle, another key element of the Mosaic worship system was the priesthood. Aaron was the original high priest, and his sons served with him. The main functions of the priest were to offer sacrifices and gifts and to bear the people before the Lord, which implies intercession.

 WORD WEALTH

Priest, *kohen.* A priest; especially a chief priest; a minister, a personal attendant, an officer; specifically the high priest descended from Aaron. The *kohen* was the Lord's "personal attendant," one whose entire life revolved around Yahweh's service, both through ministering in the tabernacle (or temple in later times) and in carrying the burden of the people of Israel (see Ex. 28:29). A *kohen* ministers to the Lord as priest (Ex. 28:1). Notice the six appearances of the words "minister," "serve," or "service" in the references to the high priest in Hebrews 8:1—9:10. To this day the Jewish surname "Cohen" identifies a family descended from Aaron the high priest.[1]

Read Leviticus 9:7. What was the priest to do for the people? What was the purpose of this action?

Comment on this high priestly aspect of Jesus' ministry (Heb. 9:11–15).

Read Exodus 28:9–12. Why was the priest to bear on his shoulders the names of the sons of Israel? What aspect of the priestly ministry does this represent?

What does the Bible say about Jesus' ministry in this regard? (Heb. 7:25)

Another type of Christ wherein we see intercession figuring prominently is in the Book of Esther.

What did Haman plan to do to the Jews? (3:8–11)

What is Haman called in Esther 3:10?

Who is the one who plans your destruction? (John 10:1–10)

How did Esther intervene for the Jews? (Esth. 4:15—5:2)

How does this parallel Jesus' intervention for us?

Once again we see many parallels of Jesus in this historic event. Just as Esther saved her people from destruction, so Jesus came to save us. Esther risked her life for her people, and Jesus gave up His life to save us. The law of the king required death for those who came into the inner court without being called; God's law also had us consigned to death, but Jesus' sacrificial approach has been accepted so that we, in Him, are delivered from the Adversary's plan for our destruction.

Perhaps one of the most remarkable pictures of Jesus in the Old Testament is in Genesis 22 where Abraham is told to sacrifice his "only son" Isaac.

 WORD WEALTH

Only son, *yachid.* An only one, an only child, a precious life. *Yachid* comes from the verb *yachad,* "to be one." *Yachid*

describes Abraham's unique miracle child, Isaac. Zechariah describes what the Messiah will one day become to Israel's repentant, weeping citizens: a previous only son (Zech. 12:10). Here the place where God told Abraham to sacrifice his son Isaac is the same place where God sacrificed *His* own Son: the hills of Moriah in Jerusalem. Equally noteworthy is that the phrase "His only begotten Son" in John 3:16 in the Hebrew New Testament is: "His Son, His *Yachid*."[2]

Read Genesis 22:1–19.

In verse 5 what statement does Abraham make that shows his faith? What did Abraham believe God would do? (See Heb. 11:17–19.)

Who carried the wood for the sacrifice? How does this parallel Jesus' death?

What does Isaac's question in verse 7 indicate about Abraham's and Isaac's past worship?

Consider the time that this trial of faith required. What expressions relating to time are found in this passage?

What did God provide for a sacrifice? Comment on how this substitution pictures Christ.

What resulted from this trial? (vv. 15–19)

Many other people and events in Scripture illustrate facets of Jesus' life and work. Joshua shows us Jesus as the Captain leading us forward into possession of the promised inheritance God has for us. Boaz, in the Book of Ruth, is a picture of Christ as the Kinsman-Redeemer who redeems the loss we have incurred through the Fall and restores us to the possibilities God intended us to have. David shows us Jesus the Conqueror, whose kingdom will not fall short of the full measure that God has for it. Time and time again, in type and symbol, we see how God was teaching mankind through the Old Testament about the Savior and all that the Savior came to do.

FAITH ALIVE

How have these types helped you to see more of Christ in the Old Testament?

What type of Christ is the most meaningful to you?

Take the types mentioned in the last paragraph and do your own study using the texts noted or your own awareness of the stories. Take time right now to thank God for opening up more of His Word to you through the ministry of His Spirit.

Joshua (Josh. 1)

Boaz (Ruth 2; 3)

David (1 Chr. 11)

---

1. *Spirit-Filled Life Bible* (Nashville, TN: Thomas Nelson Publishers, 1991), 151, 152, "Word Wealth: 5:6 priest."

2. Ibid., 36, "Word Wealth: 22:2 only son."

Lesson 5/Messianic Prophecy, Part 2 Direct Fulfillment of Old Testament Prophecies

Having examined the types of Christ in the Old Testament, we will now look at direct prophecies of His First Coming and His atoning death. As we stated earlier, part of the purpose of prophecy is to show God's foreknowledge and to show the inevitable working out of His providential plan. In these messianic prophecies we see His plan being clearly fulfilled, and whether by the working of His Spirit, or by the wrath of man, God's redemptive plan is unfolded in the life of Jesus as was foretold by the prophets.

PROPHECIES CONCERNING THE LINEAGE OF CHRIST

Read Genesis 3:15. This is called the *Protoevangelium*; it is the first proclamation of the gospel in the Bible. From the time of Adam's Fall, and even in the midst of God's pronouncing judgment on that first sin, a promise shines forth: the work of the serpent will be overcome! Answer the following questions about the *protoevangelium*.

To whom is God speaking?

Whom does the serpent represent?

Comment on the significance of the seed of the woman.

What statement implies the struggle between Jesus and Satan?

What does Revelation 12 tell us about this ongoing strife?

What does Revelation 20:9, 10 tell us about the outcome of this struggle?

From this initial promise in Genesis 3:15, which was given to all mankind through Adam, God's redemptive plan began to be worked out in history. Years later, God promised Abraham that the promise would be fulfilled through him.

Read Genesis 22:18.

What has just happened that leads God to give this promise to Abraham?

Who is the "seed" of Abraham? (Gal. 3:16)

How are the nations blessed in Abraham? (Gal. 3:13, 14)

The working of redemption, therefore, was to be through Abraham's offspring. As the father of the faithful, Abraham had a special role to be an example to those who would come to God through faith. God taught Abraham many things, and we do not know to what level of understanding he came. He did know enough to expect Isaac to be raised from the dead if he were killed at God's command (Heb. 11:17–19). Jesus said, "Abraham rejoiced to see My day" (John 8:56), so we know that Abraham certainly had a profound prophetic understanding of God and His future redemptive purposes.

Through Abraham came Isaac, Jacob (Israel), and then the twelve tribes of Israel. And to one of Israel's sons the promise was further defined.

Read Genesis 49:8–12.

To whom did Jacob give this blessing?

What statements does Jacob make indicating that the rulership of Israel would come through Judah?

Who would come to receive the ultimate obedience of the people? Whom does this signify?

WORD WEALTH

Shiloh, *shiloh.* Shiloh was a city where the tabernacle was set up (Josh. 18:1). Here in Genesis it appears to be a proper name or title, which believers generally accept as a messianic designation of Jesus. The derivation is uncertain. One idea is that *shiloh* means "the peaceful one." Another view is that *shiloh* is a noun with a pronominal suffix that should be understood to mean "his son"; thus, lawgivers and princes would not depart from Judah until his son comes. Another possibility is to divide *shiloh* into the two words *shay* and *loh,* which would mean "the one to whom tribute is brought." The most likely meaning of *shiloh* is the one accepted by most of the ancient Jewish authorities who understood *shiloh* to be a word compounded from *shel* and *loh,* meaning "to whom it belongs." *Shelloh* may be expressed by the English phrases: "to whom dominion belongs," "whose is the kingdom," "he whose right it is to reign." See especially Ezekiel 21:27.[1]

The rulership of the tribe of Judah came to fruition in King David. And it was to David that the next promise concerning Messiah's lineage came.

Read 2 Samuel 7:12–16. Verse 13 is an example of multiple fulfillment of prophecy. What two descendants of David are referred to?

Thus, in what manner did Solomon and Jesus each fulfill this prophecy?

See Ezekiel 37:24, 25. How does this verse relate to the prophecy in 2 Samuel?

Read Hebrews 1:5, 5:8, and 12:3–6. Comment on how these passages correlate with 2 Samuel 7:14.

In 2 Samuel 7:18–29, how did David respond to this prophecy?

Thus the promise came to David that the Messiah would come through his line. David's response is beautiful in its humility. He could have become puffed up thinking, "*My* line will know no end, and *my* descendant will be established as a king forever!" But this "man after God's own heart" knew that his own power and righteousness did not earn this promise. With humbleness he came to God with thanksgiving.

We have seen in these few prophecies how God's promise of a Redeemer was given to Adam, then to Abraham, Judah, and David. In other places the Lord told the prophets many other details about the coming of the Holy One.

PROPHECIES OF THE FIRST COMING

Read Isaiah 7:14, 9:6, 7, and 11:1, 2. These passages are regularly remembered at Christmastime, and they each tell us significant things about the Messiah's coming.

What specific truth does each text tell us about Jesus' coming?

Is. 7:14

Is. 9:6, 7

Is. 11:1, 2

List the five titles Jesus is given in Isaiah 9:6 and comment on how each relates to your personal life right now.

The above references are generally related to Jesus' birth. But, as we have considered them, we have seen their dual application—then and now. All of these scriptures are meant for us today, and the truths they teach are to have an impact in our daily lives. Let us consider other prophecies relating to His birth.

Read Micah 5:2 and Matthew 2:1–12. What statement in Micah 5:2 refers to Jesus being the eternal God?

"Bethlehem" means "House of Bread." Discuss the significance of that name (see John 6:25–68).

Read Hosea 11:1, 2. What is this passage *primarily* referring to?

What does Matthew 2:14, 15 relate this passage to?

What characteristic of prophecy does this illustrate?

In addition to foretelling the birth of Christ, many Old Testament prophecies tell about His ministry. When Jesus came the first time, He came meek and lowly, as a servant to mankind. Let us observe how the prophets saw this aspect of Jesus' ministry.

PROPHECIES OF CHRIST'S MINISTRY

Read Isaiah 40:11 and Ezekiel 34:11–16. To what is the Lord likened in these passages?

What three things does Isaiah say the Lord will do as a shepherd?

How many times does Ezekiel specifically say or indicate, "I will feed them"?

What else will the Lord our Shepherd do according to Ezekiel?

Notice that in verses 14 and 15 Ezekiel says both, "I will feed," and "they shall lie down." What is being communicated by these two figures?

Read Luke 15:1–7 and John 10:11–18. Comment on Jesus' use of the figure of the shepherd.

What famous passage in Psalms likens the Lord to a shepherd? Read it and note in writing the characteristics of Jesus it reveals.

 WORD WEALTH

Feed, *ra'ah.* To shepherd, feed, tend; to pasture; to cause one's herd or flock to graze. *Ra'ah* has to do with tending and caring for one's animals, particularly by providing them with good pasture. This verb occurs more than 170 times in the Old Testament. David's early duty to feed his father's flocks (1 Sam. 17:15) is followed by his later task of shepherding the heavenly Father's flock, Israel (Ps. 78:71). The participial form of *ra'ah* is *ro'eh,* "shepherd, tender of sheep, caretaker." *Ro'eh* appears in "The Lord *is* my shepherd; I shall not want" (Ps. 23:1). See also "Shepherd of Israel" in Psalm 80:1. Ezekiel 34:23 and Micah 5:4 describe the Messiah's responsibility as one of feeding and shepherding.[2]

Read Isaiah 42:1–4.

What two titles are used for Christ in verse 1?

List five characteristics of Jesus' ministry as outlined in this passage.

How does this passage minister to you and help you relate to Jesus with a greater sense of peace?

Isaiah 61:1, 2 has been called the inauguration passage of the Lord Jesus, for it was this passage that Jesus read in the synagogue in Nazareth at the beginning of His ministry. Examining this passage we can see what the ministry of Jesus was all about.

Read Isaiah 61:1, 2. Compare Luke 4:16–21.

List five things the Messiah ("Anointed One") was anointed to do.

Which one of those ministries do you need to have from Jesus today?

Notice Isaiah 61:2 and Luke 4:19. Where does Jesus cut off the quotation?

What does this suggest about the rest of the prophecy?

What characteristic of prophecy is shown by this sudden stop in the New Testament quote from the Old Testament?

 WORD WEALTH

Anointed, *mashach.* To anoint, to rub with oil, especially in order to consecrate someone or something. Appearing almost 70 times, *mashach* refers to the custom of rubbing or smearing with sacred oil to consecrate holy persons or holy things. Priests (Lev. 8:12; 16:32) and kings (2 Sam. 2:4; 5:3; 1 Kin. 1:39) in particular were installed in their offices by anointing. In Exodus 40:9–14, the tabernacle was to be anointed, as well as the altar, the laver, and the high priest's sons. The most important derivative of *mashach* is *mashiyach* (Messiah), "anointed one." As Jesus was and is the promised Anointed One, His title came to be "Jesus the Messiah." Messiah was translated into Greek as *Christos,* thus His designation, "Jesus Christ."[3]

The Anointed One came to bring freedom to *all* who were bound, and that promise was to extend beyond the boundaries of national Israel. In the following passages, note where the Lord indicates that this promise is for people of other nations as well as Israel.

Is. 62:1–3

Is. 65:1

Jer. 16:19–21

Amos 9:11, 12

Mic. 4:1, 2

 PROBING THE DEPTHS

The blessings Jesus Christ was to bring were to extend to all nations even as Abraham was promised, "In your seed all the nations of the earth shall be blessed" (Gen. 22:18). Throughout the writings of the prophets are many references to this promise, and it is easy to recognize that those promises are fulfilled through Jesus and through His church's taking the gospel to the nations. However, these prophecies were not well understood ahead of time. The early church had an ongoing debate until about A.D. 50 over the question of Gentile believers and their relationship to the Law. In A.D. 50 the first church council took place in Jerusalem (see Acts 15). The decision of the church leaders was that the current work of God was in agreement with scriptures which indicated that the Gentiles would openly respond to the Lord. In their decision, which was written to the Gentile churches, they declared that Gentiles were not obliged to keep the ritual law, but that living in faith and obedience to God's moral principles would suffice.

PROPHECIES OF CHRIST'S DEATH

The promise of redemption did extend to all nations, and, of course, the purchase of that redemption was accomplished by the culmination of Christ's work: His death and resurrection. The prophets foretold many details of His death, again showing God's ultimate control over earthly events.

Within the Psalms many prophecies concerning Christ are given as shown in the following chart. We will consider a few passages in detail which relate directly to Jesus' death.

 AT A GLANCE

THE CHRIST OF THE PSALMS[4]		
Psalm	**Portrayal**	**Fulfilled**
2:7	The Son of God	Matthew 3:17
8:2	Praised by children	Matthew 21:15, 16
8:6	Ruler of all	Hebrews 2:8
16:10	Rises from death	Matthew 28:7
22:1	Forsaken by God	Matthew 27:46
22:7, 8	Derided by enemies	Luke 23:35
22:16	Hands and feet pierced	John 20:27
22:18	Lots cast for clothes	Matthew 27:35, 36
34:20	Bones unbroken	John 19:32, 33, 36
35:11	Accused by false witnesses	Mark 14:57
35:19	Hated without cause	John 15:25
40:7, 8	Delights in God's will	Hebrews 10:7
41:9	Betrayed by a friend	Luke 22:47
45:6	The eternal King	Hebrews 1:8
68:18	Ascends to heaven	Acts 1:9–11
69:9	Zealous for God's house	John 2:17
69:21	Given vinegar and gall	Matthew 27:34
109:4	Prays for enemies	Luke 23:34
109:8	His betrayer replaced	Acts 1:20
110:1	Rules over His enemies	Matthew 22:44
110:4	A priest forever	Hebrews 5:6
118:22	The chief stone of God's building	Matthew 21:42
118:26	Comes in the name of the Lord	Matthew 21:9

Psalm 22 is remarkable in its portrayal of the Crucifixion. One thousand years before Christ, David composed this Psalm in which there are no less than eight direct references to the Crucifixion. Read all of Psalm 22 and list the references to the Crucifixion that you see.

Read Matthew 27:36–44. What does this correspond to in Psalm 22?

Read John 19:34. Describe how that correlates with Psalm 22:14.

What physical need is spoken of in Psalm 22:15? How was this fulfilled in the Crucifixion? (See John 19:28.)

How was Psalm 22:16 fulfilled? Find and list references.

Read Mark 15:24. What part of Psalm 22 is fulfilled herein?

When people were crucified, one result of the weight of the body being suspended in that fashion was that the bones would become disjointed. Where does Psalm 22 predict this?

Verse 1 of Psalm 22 was spoken by Jesus on the Cross. God cannot look upon sin, and as Jesus took our sin upon Himself, the Father turned away. The fellowship that the Father and the Son enjoyed from before worlds existed was sundered at that moment. We cannot conceive of the magnitude of that separation, when the judgment of God—separating Himself from sin—was being borne by the Son. But Hebrews 12:2 tells us that Jesus endured the Cross "for the joy that was set before Him." The separation from God that

Jesus experienced was borne because of His love for us and the joy He has in restoring us to the Father.

Another fact of the Crucifixion that was foretold in Psalms related to Jesus' bones not being broken.

Read Psalm 34:20 and John 19:32–36. What were the circumstances surrounding the fulfillment of this prophecy?

Recalling that the Passover is a type of Christ's work, read Exodus 12:46 and Numbers 9:12. Comment on the relationship of these texts to Psalm 34:20.

Throughout the writings of the prophets are many references to Jesus' death and the events leading up to it. His betrayal, in particular, is mentioned several times. Look at the following references and tell what aspect of Jesus' betrayal is foretold.

Ps. 41:9

Zech. 11:12, 13

Many other references are made to the Passion and Crucifixion. Look at the following texts and discuss how they relate to the Passion.

Is. 50:6

Zech. 12:10

Zech. 13:1

Zech. 13:6

Find references in each of the Gospels that show Isaiah 50:6 being fulfilled.

Along with Psalm 22, one of the greatest concentrations of prophecies concerning Jesus' death is found in Isaiah 53. In this great passage specific details of Jesus' death are given. Beyond that, much is said about the significance of Jesus' death and the provisions it has made for us. Let us study this passage together.

Read Isaiah 52:13—53:12. Cite where the following details of the Passion are foretold in this passage.

The Lord was despised (Mark 15:31, 32).

The Lord was scourged (John 19:1).

The Lord was silent before His accusers (Mark 15:3–5).

The Lord died with sinners (Luke 23:32, 33).

The Lord was buried in a rich man's tomb (Matt. 27:57–60).

Where in this passage does it indicate that this atonement would extend to all nations?

In verse 5 what four specific provisions for us are listed?

List the phrases in this passage that indicate Jesus would suffer for our sins.

This passage provides a detailed look at the work of Christ and its meaning for us, but we cannot overlook the finale of Christ's work. Without the Resurrection, the plan of God would have been unfulfilled. This, too, He revealed to His prophets.

Read the following texts and comment on their fulfillment in the Resurrection.

Ps. 16:10

Hos. 13:14

John 2:18–22

 FAITH ALIVE

Looking at God's work as it was revealed to the prophets and fulfilled in Jesus, we develop a greater trust and confidence in the Lord and in His commitment to His Word (see Ps. 138:2). So we can trust His promises to us, including the promise of His return.

What promises of God are you waiting to see fulfillment of?

What aspect of Christ's work needs to be applied to your life today?

1. *Spirit-Filled Life Bible* (Nashville, TN: Thomas Nelson Publishers, 1991), 77, "Word Wealth: 49:10 Shiloh."
2. Ibid., 1012, "Word Wealth: 40:11 feed."
3. Ibid., 1043, "Word Wealth: 61:1 anointed."
4. Ibid., 772, Chart: "The Christ of the Psalms."

Lesson 6/The Fact of the Second Coming

A few years ago, a group of liberal Protestant scholars convened to discuss the Second Coming of Christ. After long discussions they determined: (1) that Jesus did not promise to return literally, (2) that the New Testament did not support a literal, physical coming of Christ, and (3) that the early creeds did not evidence a belief in the Second Coming.

Of course, the happy truth of the gospel is that they were wrong on all three counts! Turn and read 2 Peter 3:3, 4. What are we told about such attitudes?

Unbelief will always lift its cynical mocking, but in this lesson we will examine the evidence, both biblical and extra-biblical, that proclaims the fact of the Second Coming. Thus, let us stabilize and strengthen our conviction: *Jesus is coming again*!

THE SECOND COMING IN THE OLD TESTAMENT

The Second Coming is a foundational Christian belief. It has been called the "blessed hope" (Titus 2:13) of the New Testament believer. But the prophecies of the Second Coming reach back into the Old Testament, also, for the coming of Messiah in power and glory was part of their hope as well.

Before we look at some of these prophecies, let's recall a few things we have learned about prophecy.

In lesson 2 we examined characteristics of the nature of prophecy. A key characteristic is that prophecy is discursive; therefore, the prophets themselves were not always aware of how the pieces of their prophecy fit together. Thus, when the prophets saw the coming of the Messiah they sometimes overlapped elements of His first and second comings without realizing that what they seemed to see as one would be *two* events as the promise became fully realized through time. We can look back now and recognize this separation in time of the two "advents" or "comings of Christ."

Read Isaiah 40:1–11.

Who was the fulfillment of verses 3, 4? (See Matt. 3:1–3; Mark 1:2–4; Luke 3:1–6; and John 1:19–23.)

The fulfillment of Isaiah 40:5 was (or will be) when? (Don't forget multiple fulfillment of prophecy.)

Consider verses 6–8. What does this passage say to you?

Verse 10 is probably referring to what? (See Rev. 22:12.)

Which coming of Christ does Isaiah 40:11 prophesy?

Here we have a good example of the manner in which the Old Testament prophets spoke of the coming Messiah. Within this short passage we have reference (1) to Christ's dying-atoning work during His first advent (vv. 1, 2); (2) to the messenger who would proclaim the coming of the Lord; (3) to other references that could refer to the First Coming, the Second Coming, or both; and (4) in the midst of it all, a meditation contrasting the transience of man with the steadfast surety of God's Word. Such combinations could make this passage confusing, but understanding prophecy's discursive nature helps us see that the primary message of the passage was *comfort* when the Redeemer comes. Rather than a systematic exposition of the coming of God's Messiah, we see glimpses of His glory amid promises of His plan to be unveiled. Let's look at other illustrations of the mixing of the first and second coming in some other Old Testament prophets.

The Book of Zechariah is perhaps the most messianic book in the Old Testament, and we have seen that it contains numerous prophecies that were fulfilled in Jesus' life and ministry. Some of those prophecies contain this same mixture of aspects of Christ's first and second comings; other seem to focus exclusively on the coming of Messiah in victory, which we recognize as being future. Let us examine some of Zechariah's prophecies.

Read Zechariah 8:3–8.

What significance is related to the Lord's "return" in verse 3?

When will the prophecy of the Lord's ruling in peace from Jerusalem be fulfilled? (vv. 4, 5)

What will happen? (vv. 7, 8)

This passage speaks of things we have not yet seen historically fulfilled, yet we properly and wisely assume that its fulfillment is future. When? Well, the time when one believes this prophecy is fulfilled depends upon the prophetic system he or she espouses. In future lessons we will be considering various schemes of prophetic interpretation and how these prophecies fit into them. For the present it is sufficient to simply see the Old Testament foretelling of a victorious coming of Christ, which we recognize as the Second Coming.

Read Zechariah 9:9, 10.

Was this whole passage fulfilled in one event?

Explain this passage and its fulfillment in light of what we have studied.

Here again we see that the prophet saw the coming of the King, yet he did not perceive the gap in time that existed between verses 9 and 10.

Read Zechariah 14:3, 4.

Where does it say the Lord will stand?

Comment on this passage, noting dual fulfillments and time lapse in light of Acts 1:9–12.

Other prophets also spoke of Jesus' Second Coming. In keeping with the prophets' view of the Day of the Lord and their view of the dual aspects of judgment, they saw the Second Coming in terms of both wrath and salvation.

Read Haggai 2:6–9. Which aspect of judgment is foretold?

The temple spoken of here was built after the Exile, and it was the same temple which Herod the Great helped to expand and beautify. That being the case, who visited that temple and how does that fact fulfill the prophecy that "the glory of this latter temple shall be greater than the former"? (See John 2:13–22.)

Considering the above, comment on multiple fulfillment of Malachi 3:1–3. How might this example of multiple fulfillment of prophecy yet be fulfilled? First, list which parts of this prophecy have been fulfilled and how they were fulfilled.

Second, list which parts of this prophecy are yet to be fulfilled. State how you believe it will be fulfilled in general terms. Give supporting or parallel references if possible.

THE SECOND COMING IN JESUS' TEACHING

The Old Testament prophets foretold the Second Coming as they did the First. In many instances differentiation between the two comings was cloudy or nonexistent for the Old Testament prophets, but by seeing the First Coming fulfilled we can get a better grasp on the Second Coming. In addition, we have the words of Jesus and the writings of the apostles, which give us clearer teaching on the Second Coming.

However, even with additional teaching we must not assume that we have mastered the truth of the Second Coming. Knowing the promise keeps us watchful, while a Pharisee-like presumption of "knowing the times" can lull to sleep. In our next lessons we will look in more detail at varying interpretation of Scripture with reference to the Second Coming and last things. We will see that many details of the Second Coming and surrounding events are unclear. But we cannot let our debate over detail obscure the great fact that our Lord Jesus Christ *is* returning for His church! And that "blessed hope" promise has been given us by Jesus Himself.

Read and compare side by side Matthew 16:24–27, Mark 8:34–38, and Luke 9:23–26.

What is the theme of these passages?

How will one "find" or "save" his life?

How does Jesus characterize this generation in Mark?

What three basic facts are stated about Jesus' coming in all three of these texts?

1.

2.

3.

Here we have assurance of Jesus' Coming. Jesus does not just speak of a "spiritual" coming, as though He was coming as some kind of a mystical, invisible, or ethereal presence. No! His coming will be literal, physical, and visible! He will come in glory with the angels, and He will bring judgment, rewarding each according to His works. *HE* said so!

Read Matthew 10:16–26.

To whom is Jesus speaking in this passage, and what was the occasion?

What types of things does Jesus predict the apostles will face?

What does Jesus say in this text about His coming?

Read Luke 17:20–37.

What does Jesus say will happen before "the days" of the Son of Man?

What do verses 34–36 tell us about Jesus' Coming?

What warning might we receive?

Going deeper, in Luke 17:26 and 28, to the times of which two Old Testament figures does Jesus compare the time of His return? Use your concordance or your Bible's center-column index. Look up these settings and list some characteristics of those times and how they compare to ours.

In these passages Jesus again makes clear that His coming will be a historic event. He speaks of particular things that will happen prior to His return, characteristics of the time of His return, and particular results of His coming. All these state-ments indicate that He had a literal, historic event in mind when He spoke of His return.

Jesus also taught His disciples about His return through parables. Read the following two parables and discuss their pri-mary message.

Read Matthew 25:1–13 and Luke 12:35–40.

What is the primary message of these parables?

What other lessons can be learned from these parables?

We have seen that the Second Coming is assured. But as sure as the Second Coming is, it is equally sure that we do not know exactly *when* it is. This indefiniteness keeps a disciple humble and dependent. Jesus told us two primary things to do until He comes: 1) watch and be ready, and 2) occupy until He comes. In either case, a definite knowledge of the time of His return would tempt some to carelessness. We are all human enough to put off responsibilities until we reach a deadline. But by not giving us a deadline and by teaching the imminence of His return, Jesus helps motivate us to live con-tinually in that hope, and to center our hope in our love for Him rather than in a promised date on a calendar.

However, though the uncertainty of the exact time of His return is clearly taught in Scripture, foolish people have still tried to establish the exact date of His coming. Let us examine a few more passages that remind us of the unknowableness of the time of His return, so we will not be trapped by the promises or publications of such deluded people.

Read Matthew 24:36 and Mark 13:32, 33.

According to these passages, list the people who do not know when the Son is returning.

Who does know when the Son is returning?

What three things should be done since we do not know the time of Christ's return?

1.

2.

3

Jesus made many other statements concerning His return, but perhaps the most tender, most comforting promise of His return was given to the apostles at the Last Supper.

Read John 14:1–3.

According to verse 1, what is the basis for our peace?

What is Jesus leaving to do?

Where is Jesus preparing a place?

Why is Jesus preparing a place?

This promise has been a source of comfort to Christians throughout the centuries, and His promise is so much nearer today. Let us look up in expectant hope!

THE SECOND COMING IN THE REST OF THE NEW TESTAMENT

After the death and resurrection of Jesus, The Lord taught His followers for forty days about the kingdom of God (Acts 1:3). Yet even on the day of His ascension the disciples still did not fully understand the mission they were being given. They still thought Jesus was going to set up an earthly kingdom (Acts 1:6–8). Jesus told them one last time that they were to be witnesses, and then He ascended. It may have only been at that moment that the true nature of their assignment began to become clear to them. It was also at that moment, right as Jesus left, that the disciples received confirmation of His return.

Read Acts 1:9–11.

Who spoke to the disciples?

In what manner did the angels say He would return?

Seeing that Jesus' ascension was a literal, physical, historic event, what will His return be like?

The promises of the Old Testament and from Jesus' own lips were confirmed by angels. And the expectation of His return immediately became part of the teaching and preaching of the church.

Read Acts 3:19–21. Comment on the promise of Christ's return as spoken of in this passage.

Here we see that, from the earliest preaching of the apostles, the promise of Christ's return was part of the doctrine of the church. The return of Jesus is commonly called the *parousia*; it is spoken of numerous times in the New Testament.

 WORD WEALTH

Coming, *parousia.* The technical term signifying the second advent of Jesus was never used to describe His first coming. *Parousia* originally was the official term for a visit by a person of high rank, especially a king. It was an arrival that included a permanent presence from that time onward. The glorified Messiah's arrival will be followed by a permanent residence with His glorified people.[1]

Read 1 Corinthians 15:22–24. This is a key passage dealing with the Resurrection, but it also affirms the Second Coming. Christ is declared to be the firstfruits of the Resurrection; when do believers experience the promise of the resurrection?

Read 1 John 3:2, 3.

In light of the previous passage we read, what is this text referring to?

When will the believer "be like Him"?

What action do those take who are looking forward in hope?

Read Titus 2:11–14. What parallels do you see between this text and 1 John 3:2, 3?

In all these passages we see the common threads of our hope of glorification at His coming and our striving for purity in view of that hope. When the Lord comes we shall be endued with a glorified body, and whether that means we are "raised in incorruption" (1 Cor. 15:42) or we are "changed . . . in the twinkling of an eye" (1 Cor. 15:52), it is a hope for which "we ourselves groan within ourselves" (Rom. 8:23). This purifying of ourselves is a natural outgrowth of this hope so that we may "not be ashamed before Him at His Coming" (1 John 2:28).

Some of the most extensive teaching on the Second Coming is in Paul's letters to the Thessalonians. Let us look together at some of those references.

Read 1 Thessalonians 3:12, 13.

What is Paul's prayer for the Thessalonians?

Correlate this passage with 1 John 3:2, 3.

Who is coming with Christ according to 1 Thessalonians 3:12, 13?

Here we again see the desire for purity or holiness to be worked in the church as we await the Lord's coming. But we also see the wickedness in the world becoming more gross even as the church purifies herself. The fate of the wicked at Christ's coming is also revealed.

Read 2 Thessalonians 1:9–12 and 2:8.

Who is being discussed in 1:9?

Who is being discussed in 2:8?

What is the fate of these unbelievers?

In contrast, what is Paul's prayer for the believers? (1:11, 12)

One of the most well-known passages concerning the Second Coming is in Paul's letters to the Thessalonians. Time and again "hope" is the key word we find in discussing our view of the Second Coming. This hope is to be a comfort to us.

Read 1 Thessalonians 4:13–18.

What three things will announce the return of the Lord?

What two things will happen in response?

How do you know you are ready to go? (Read 2 Tim. 4:8 and Jude 24.)

THE FACT OF THE SECOND COMING IN THE CREEDS

We have seen that the clear testimony of scripture verifies the literal, physical, historic return of Jesus Christ. Likewise, the teachings of the church throughout history have upheld this doctrine. In this last section of this lesson, we will see examples from various creeds of the church of Jesus that the steadfast teaching through the centuries has supported this doctrine.

The Apostles Creed

I believe in God the Father Almighty; Maker of heaven and earth.

And in Jesus Christ his only begotten Son our Lord; who was conceived by the Holy Ghost, born of the Virgin Mary; suffered under Pontius Pilate, was crucified, dead, and buried; he descended into hell; the third day he rose from the dead; he ascended into heaven; and sitteth at the right hand of God the Father Almighty; from thence he shall come to judge the quick and the dead.

I believe in the Holy Ghost; the holy catholic Church; the communion of saints; the forgiveness of sins; the resurrection of the body; and the life everlasting. Amen.[2]

What phrases assert the promise of Christ's return?

Now, notice these words as they have been repeated in successive generations.

The Nicene Creed (Excerpted)

I believe . . . in one Lord Jesus Christ, the only begotten Son of God . . . he shall come again, with glory, to judge both the quick and the dead; whose kingdom shall have no end.[3]

The Athanasian Creed (Excerpted)

39. He [Jesus] ascended into heaven, he sitteth on the right hand of the Father God Almighty.

40. From whence he shall come to judge the quick and the dead.[4]

The Augsburg Confession (Excerpted)

Article 3, paragraph 3

The same Christ shall openly come again, to judge the quick and the dead, according as the Apostles' Creed declareth and other things.[5]

The Westminister Shorter Catechism (Excerpted)

Question 28. Wherein consisteth Christ's exaltation?

Answer. Christ's exaltation consisteth in his rising again from the dead on the third day, in ascending up into heaven, in sitting at the right hand of God the Father, and in coming to judge the world at the last day.[6]

New Hampshire Baptist Confession
(Excerpted)

XVIII. Of the World to Come

We believe that the end of the world is approaching; that at the last day Christ will descend from heaven, and raise the dead from the grave to final retribution; that a solemn separation will then take place; that the wicked will be adjudged to endless punishment, and the righteous to endless joy; and that this judgment will fix forever the final state of men in heaven or hell, on principles of righteousness.[7]

Read the following triumphant declaration of faith in the second coming of Christ as set forth by the Foursquare Church. It is representative of many present-day evangelical congregations:

We believe that the Second Coming of Christ is personal and imminent; that He will descend from Heaven in the clouds of glory with the voice of the archangel and with the trump of God; and that at this hour, which no man knoweth beforehand, the dead in Christ shall rise, then the redeemed that are alive and remain shall be caught up together with them in the clouds, to meet the Lord in the air, and that so shall they be with the Lord; that also seeing that a thousand years is as a day with the Lord, and that no man knoweth the hour of His appearance, which we believe to be near at hand, each day should be lived as though He were expected to appear at even, yet in that obedience to His explicit command, "Occupy till I come," the work of spreading the Gospel, the sending forth of missionaries, and the general duties for the upbuilding of the Church should be carried on as diligently, and thoroughly, as though neither ours nor the next generation should live in the flesh to that glorious day.

Thus we see that throughout the history of the church, from the words of Jesus to the present time, believers all over

the world have held the hope of Christ's return as a sure doctrine of Scripture.

 FAITH ALIVE

Knowing that Jesus could return at any time, how
should we conduct our lives?

In what way will the stirring up of this hope help you to
purify yourself?

Ask the Holy Spirit to bring His holy flame to bear upon
any area of your life that needs purifying, and ask the Lord of
the harvest to send forth laborers, for *"the* night is coming
when no one can work"* (John 9:4).

1. *Spirit-Filled Life Bible* (Nashville, TN: Thomas Nelson Publishers, 1991), 1744,
"Word Wealth: 15:23 coming."
2. Philip Schaff, *The Creeds of Christendom* (New York, NY: Harper and Brothers,
1877), II, 45.
3. Ibid., II, 58.
4. Ibid., II, 66.
5. Ibid., III, 9.
6. Ibid., III, 681.
7. Ibid., III, 748.

Lesson 7/The Olivet Discourse and Views of the Rapture

"Daddy, what will happen when Jesus comes back?" As long as she had been alive three-year-old Katie had heard her father pray for his family to be ready for Jesus' return.

Her father's mind spun through arguments about Pre-Trib Rapture or Post-Trib Rapture interspersed with pictures of people rising in the air and runaway cars suddenly bereft of drivers. How do you explain this to a three-year-old?

"Katie," her father answered, "there's a lot we don't know about when and how Jesus will come back, but we love Him and we want to be with Him."

"Yes. But Dad," asked Katie, "will teddy bear go with me?"

Her father laughed gently, "I don't know, Katie, but I know we will be happy to be with Jesus."

To a three-year-old the most important question about the Rapture might be whether her teddy bear will go with her, but for many others the debate can become quite heated. Like Katie's father, we do well to keep foremost in our minds that there is much that we do not know—about the Rapture and about the end times in general.

In this and succeeding chapters we will be considering end times prophecy. These prophecies we will be studying are interpreted from several different viewpoints. In an overview such as this, we cannot hope to thoroughly cover every aspect of every point of view, but we do hope to cover the major interpretive schemes and the primary biblical support they cite.

As we showed in the previous chapter, the Second Coming of Christ is a fact well attested to by Scripture and forms a basic part of the historic beliefs of the church. The rapture of the church is one aspect of the Second Coming, but differences in interpretation as to how the various aspects of the Second Coming fit together lead to varying views of the Rapture.

The word "rapture" does not appear in Scripture, but the primary idea is being "caught up." The main text that refers to the church's being "caught up" is in 1 Thessalonians 4:13–18.

Read this passage and tell why Paul wrote it. (v. 13)

What two groups of people will meet the Lord? (vv. 15, 17)

What other information is given about this meeting: Where is it? What is its duration? What announces it?

 WORD WEALTH

Caught up, *harpadzo.* To seize, snatch away, catch up, take by force. The word describes the Holy Spirit's action in transferring Philip from one location to another (Acts 8:39) and Paul's being caught up to Paradise (2 Cor. 12:2, 4). It suggests the exercise of a sudden force.[1]

So the Rapture may be defined as the event wherein the believers who are alive at the coming of the Lord are caught up to meet the Lord in the air. The Rapture is actually one of a number of events which relate to the Second Coming; however, it is often the single event most commonly associated with the promise of Jesus' return. To fit the pieces together, let's study Jesus' own teaching about His coming.

Jesus' greatest prophetic teaching is called the Olivet Discourse, because this teaching occasion with the disciples occurred on the Mount of Olives. The fullest record of that teaching is found in Matthew 24 and 25, although parallel passages are in Mark 13 and Luke 21.

Read Matthew 24:1–3.

What does Jesus prophesy in verse 2?

What three questions do the disciples ask? (v. 3)

It is important to see from the beginning that Jesus is answering three questions; He is not only speaking of His "coming," but also of "these things" (v. 2—the destroyed temple) and "the end of the age" (the climax of this era).

Read Matthew 24:1–51 and note the divisions as Jesus deals with (1) the destruction of Jerusalem, (2) His coming, and (3) "the end."

List five signs that Jesus calls "the beginning of sorrows" in verses 4–8.

Read Matthew 24:9–14.

In verse 9 does "then" mean "afterward" or "during that time"?

What types of things does Jesus speak of in this section?

What will happen before the end comes?

When Jesus says "then the end will come," He is speaking of the end of what?

Read Matthew 24:15–28.

This passage is another probable example of multiple fulfillment of prophecy. Jesus refers to the destruction of Jerusalem by the Romans in A.D. 70. Could His language also point to the times leading up to His return? Look again at verses 15–22. Explain how this text could apply to the Roman destruction of Jerusalem.

What indications are there that the text refers to more than just the earlier Roman attack on Jerusalem?

Who are the "elect"? (To accept the challenge of this interpretive matter, look at different groups/individuals called "elect"—Rom. 11:1–5; 9:11; 2 Tim. 2:10; 2 Pet. 1:10.)

Reread Matthew 24:23–28. Compare these verses with verses 5 and 11, and note common points.

Could these separate references be referring to the same thing?

Read Matthew 24:29–31.

What is prophesied in this passage?

What does verse 31 in particular refer to?

It is important to pause here and examine this text as it bears on the Rapture. Verse 21 of this chapter refers to "great tribulation," and several of the major views of the Rapture center on the timing of the Rapture as it occurs in relationship to the Great Tribulation. In these prophetic systems, the Great Tribulation is regarded as a seven-year period of judgment on the earth. The church is viewed as either being raptured prior to this judgment, or as being on earth for part of it, or as living through the entire Tribulation and surviving victoriously through persecution. Note that this text seems to support a "post-tribulation" rapture. That is, if the "great tribulation" in verse 21 is the seven-year period of judgment, then verses 29–31 indicate that Christ's coming and the Rapture are "immediately after the tribulation of those days" (v. 29).

Another view of this passage sees the Tribulation, not as a consummating seven-year judgment, but as an age-long event. This idea suggests that the "great tribulation" is the full duration of the church's witness, wherein the signs of which Jesus speaks grow in frequency and intensity as the end of this age nears. Thus "immediately after the tribulation of those days" just means near or at the very end of the age.

Read Matthew 24:32–35.

In verses 32 and 33 what two things does Jesus parallel as an illustration?

What are "all these things" which Jesus refers to in verse 33?

When Jesus says "this generation" in verse 34, what generation is He speaking of? Are there other possible interpretations of what generation that is?

The fig tree is often seen as a symbol of Israel. Seen in that light, verse 32 becomes a prophecy of the rebirth of the state of Israel, and that is a legitimate interpretation of verse 32. However, it is important to see that Jesus was making a comparison or drawing a parallel. He said that one can observe the fig tree and know the season; likewise one can see "these things [signs]" and know that the Second Coming is near.

Read Matthew 24:36–44.

What is the primary message of this passage?

How many times does Jesus reiterate that we do not know the time of His coming?

This passage is an interesting contrast to the preceding passage. In verses 32–35 Jesus has just told us that we will see the signs and know that His coming is near—"at the doors" (v. 33). He then turns around and says that no one knows the hour or the day, and we must be prepared, for that day will come unexpectedly. It is instructive to note the verbs that are used in these passages: verse 33 tells us we will *see* the signs; verse 42 tells us to *watch* for His coming. It is too easy for us to get caught up in what is happening in the world and how it might fulfill prophecy. We might end up *watching* for the signs instead of *watching* for Jesus. Jesus said we would *see* the signs, but we must *watch* for Him—*HE* is to always remain the focus of our attention.

This passage also speaks of the days of Noah as a parallel to the time of Jesus' coming. This illustration may be seen as support for either the Pre-Tribulation or Pre-Wrath Rapture view. Proponents of those views point out that Noah and his family were removed before the judgment was poured out on the earth. It is also interesting to note that Noah was in the Ark seven days before the Flood came. Some suggest that this could represent the seven years in which believers are with the Lord before the final visitation of God's wrath upon the earth. So some elements of a prophecy may be interpreted as suggested, and thereby applied as support for a given view.

Read Matthew 24:45–51.

How does Jesus describe the first servant?

How does the first servant rule the household?

What reward will he obtain at his master's return?

How does the evil servant rule the household?

What is his reward?

Read Matthew 25:1–13.

What is the message of this parable?

What does oil represent in the Bible? (See 1 John 2:20, 27.)

The Holy Spirit is generally typified by oil in the Scriptures. In that light, what lesson should we learn from the oil in this parable?

Read Matthew 25:14–30.

Why did the master give varying amounts to the three servants?

How did the master respond to the two servants who multiplied their talents?

What difference was there in his response to those two servants?

What did the third servant do with his talent?

Why did the third servant hide his talent?

What was his reward?

In these three parables Jesus teaches us about how we should be watching for His return, and He gives two important lessons. On one hand, we must watch in earnest expectation of His return. On the other hand, we are told to do business and extend His kingdom until His return. These two ideas are not in opposition; they must be married in our understanding.

Describe how the three parables just studied teach the two lessons of watching earnestly and carrying on business.

How would you apply each parable to your own life?

Read Matthew 25:31–46.

What six things does Jesus say that the righteous did for Him?

How is this passage similar to the preaching of the Old Testament prophets?

In this passage Christ's final judgment of the nations is discussed. In keeping with the traditional message of Old Testament prophetic preaching, He discusses our treatment of the poor and oppressed and the caring for those victims of injustice as an element in the judgment.

From Jesus' teaching we can see that there are manifest signs leading up to His return, the believers will be taken to be with Him at His return, and He will judge the world after His return. These things are generally agreed upon. The manner in which they actually occur is not agreed upon, and we have seen how various portions of the Olivet Discourse can be used to support at least three different views of the Rapture. Let us look closer now at the views of the Rapture.

VIEWS OF THE RAPTURE

In the following chart some basic questions are answered for five different views of the Rapture. It is important to note that these five views are charted in a representative way, not an exhaustive way. There are many views that combine various elements of these five positions in different ways, but most views will fall into one of these five categories.

	Pre-Tribulation Rapture	Mid-Tribulation Rapture	Post-Tribulation Rapture	Partial Rapture	Pre-Wrath Rapture
Is there a literal 7-year Tribulation?	Yes	Yes	Yes	Yes	No
Are the Rapture and the Second Coming separate events?	Yes	Yes	No	Yes	Yes
When is the Rapture?	Before Tribulation	In the middle of the Tribulation	After Tribulation	Before Tribulation	Before the outpouring of God's Wrath
When is the Second Coming?	After Tribulation	After Tribulation	After Tribulation	After Tribulation	After the outpouring of God's Wrath

A concept that is central to all of these views is that God's wrath will not be poured out upon believers. The key text supporting that proposition is found in 1 Thessalonians 5.

Read 1 Thessalonians 5:1–11.

What has Paul just finished speaking about at the end of chapter 4?

How does Paul describe the coming of the "day of the Lord" in verse 2?

What does Paul say in verse 4 about our awareness as believers?

What should our attitude be as "sons of the day"?

What does verse 9 tell us about the wrath of God?

In this passage Paul tells us we are not appointed to wrath, and he is speaking in the context of the "day of the Lord." (Remember our lesson 3 study.) To some degree all views of the Rapture depend on this verse; their differences come from how each position views what is meant by "wrath" and when it occurs.

THE PRE-TRIBULATION RAPTURE VIEW

The Pre-Tribulation Rapture view sees the wrath of God as being a seven-year Great Tribulation. We saw one reference to "great tribulation" as we studied the Olivet Discourse. The only other biblical reference containing the expression "great tribulation" is in Revelation 7:14.

Read Revelation 7:9–17 and consider the following questions.

Who is the multitude?

Where is the multitude?

What information does the passage give us about the Great Tribulation?

WORD WEALTH

Tribulation, *thlipsis.* Pressure, oppression, stress, anguish, tribulation, adversity, affliction, crushing, squashing, squeezing, distress. Imagine placing your hand on a stack of loose items and manually compressing them. That is *thlipsis,* putting a lot of pressure on that which is free and unfettered. *Thlipsis* is like spiritual bench-pressing. The word is used of crushing grapes or olives in a press.[2]

Another phrase that is sometimes identified as the Tribulation is "the time of Jacob's trouble." This phrase is found only in Jeremiah 30:7.

Recalling the key themes in Old Testament prophecy, what is "that day" in Jeremiah 30:7 referring to?

What does this verse say supporting the Pre-Tribulation Rapture view?

From these references we see that biblical support is given for the Pre-Tribulation Rapture view, but to some extent one must decide that the Rapture occurs first and these verses apply to being saved by means of the Rapture from the Tribulation rather than it being explicitly stated in the Bible that this sequence of events occurs. As we look at other views we will see that the same can be said for them as well.

THE MID-TRIBULATION RAPTURE VIEW

This view also sees the Great Tribulation as being a seven-year period of judgment on the earth, but unlike the Pre-Tribulation Rapture view, this view sees the Rapture occurring three-and-a-half years into the Tribulation. Various prophecies indicate that people will be martyred for their faith in Jesus during the Tribulation, and it is this fact that the Mid-Tribulation Rapture view tries to reconcile with the overall prophetic scheme.

Read Revelation 6:9–11.

According to these verses, what did John see?

Why were the people martyred?

Does this represent all martyrs? Why?

Read Revelation 13:1–8.

What does this prophecy relate to?

How long does the beast have "authority to continue"?

Do you see this period of time as literal or figurative? Why?

What does the beast do to the saints?

We see here clear evidence that people are martyred during the time which is considered by these prophetic systems to be the Great Tribulation. In the Mid-Tribulation Rapture view the persecution of the saints lasts forty-two months (three and one-half years) and then the Rapture occurs. Pre-Tribulation Rapture proponents claim that the martyrs spoken of in these passages are those who come to Christ during the Tribulation. Other views see the time period as symbolic rather than specific.

THE PARTIAL RAPTURE VIEW

This view attempts to reconcile the martyrdom of saints during the Tribulation by suggesting that not all believers are taken in the Rapture. According to this view, believers who are not ready to meet the Lord when He comes are left on earth to prove their faithfulness by being martyred. They cite the parable of the Ten Virgins as support for this view.

Read Matthew 25:1–13. Explain how this parable is interpreted to support the Partial Rapture view.

THE POST-TRIBULATION RAPTURE VIEW

We have already seen one supporting text for the Post-Tribulation Rapture view in our study of the Olivet Discourse. In addition, there obviously is no problem determining who the martyred believers are if the Rapture does not occur until the end of the Great Tribulation.

According to this view the Rapture and Jesus' second coming to earth are one event. The believers are caught up to meet the Lord in the air as He returns. Then the Lord and His saints immediately descend to the earth and rule the earth during the Millennium. Some who hold this view are fond of pointing out that the teachings of the church throughout history have supported one Second Coming, not a Second Coming that is split up into two or more parts. This is true, but we must also recognize that the Jews thought there would only be one coming of the Messiah as well. Many of the religious leaders of Jesus' day missed their Messiah because He did not fit into their prophetic plans. In studying prophecy we must always remain humble and nondogmatic, recognizing that none of us can truly say that our system is infallible. What *is* infallible is God's Word, and the consistent and sure message we have from God's Word is: Jesus is coming back, so watch and be ready!

PRE-WRATH RAPTURE VIEW

This view breaks away from the others in that it does not view the Great Tribulation as being a literal seven-year period. (Some variations of this view do work with a seven-year tribulation through which believers live until just prior to the final outpouring of God's wrath.) According to this view, most of the tribulation signs are things which occur throughout the church age, but they grow more frequent and intense as the end nears.

In this view believers are delivered from God's wrath as stated in 1 Thessalonians 5:9. But this view sees God's wrath, not as the entire Tribulation period, but as a brief, intense period of judgment at the very end.

Read Revelation 6:12–17; 11:15–19; 16:17–21.

List common elements in these three judgments.

Considering the similarities of these texts, could they overlap in a way so as to actually be one and the same event viewed from different perspectives by the prophet?

How does each passage refer to God's wrath?

Read Revelation 15:1 and 16:1.

What plagues or judgments do these passages refer to?

What does 15:1 say which might indicate that these plagues are uniquely the wrath of God?

We have seen that none of these views can claim to have a complete, airtight lock on the truth. In each case one's own interpretive outlook will influence how one judges the various views and which view one espouses. We can, however, remain united in our blessed hope of our Savior's return, realizing that when we are all around the throne, worshiping God in heaven, no one will really care what view of the Rapture that another held.

---

1. *Spirit-Filled Life Bible* (Nashville, TN: Thomas Nelson Publishers, 1991), 1830, "Word Wealth: 4:17 caught up."
2. Ibid., 1607, "Word Wealth: 16:33 tribulation."

Lesson 8/Views of Revelation

The newspaper advertisement arrested Jim's attention instantly: "PROPHECY SEMINAR—ARE WE NOW IN THE TIME OF THE FOURTH SEAL?" Jim showed his friend Bill.

"Can you believe this?" Jim exclaimed. "Don't these people know that the seals aren't opened until after the Rapture?"

"Well," responded Bill, "I don't think the seals will be opened one at a time like this implies, but the seals are almost all open now."

"Haven't you read the Bible? The Bible clearly says that the Rapture comes before the Great Tribulation!" said Jim emphatically.

"I'm not sure what you mean by the Great Tribulation. It seems to me that there's plenty of tribulation in the world now, and a lot of what Revelation talks about seems to be happening," Bill replied.

"But Revelation is about the future!" shouted Jim.

"Don't get upset!" said Bill, "Let's ask Tom. He knows a lot about the Bible."

When they found Tom they asked him if he thought that the Rapture had to happen before the events of Revelation were to happen.

"Why, of course not," said Tom, "Most of Revelation was fulfilled in the first-century church."

Revelation is a confusing book to many people, and it can become more perplexing if we do not realize that there are several different interpretive approaches to the book. In this lesson we will discuss aspects of the Tribulation and Second

Coming. However, we will be discussing those topics from within the framework of interpretive systems relating to the Book of Revelation.

There are five primary categories into which interpretive approaches to Revelation fall. Before we examine these approaches in detail, let's get an overview of how these basic views look at Revelation.

 BEHIND THE SCENES

Many devoted Christians are surprised to discover that other equally dedicated believers view the prophecies of the Book of Revelation differently from them. This book tolerates a wide spectrum of approaches, but the common denominator of all is the ultimate triumph of Jesus Christ, who culminates history with His final coming and reigns with and through His church forever.

The most popularized and widely discussed approach is called the *Dispensationalist* interpretation. This proposes that the Rapture of the church is referred to in Revelation 4:1, at which time the redeemed in Christ are translated into heaven at His coming "in the air" (1 Thess. 4:17). Revelation 6—18 are perceived as the Great Tribulation (Matt. 24:21) or the wrath of God (1 Thess. 5:9) from which believers are kept (Rev. 3:10). This approach sees national Israel as God's people on earth at this time (the church having been raptured), restored to Jerusalem, protected by divine seal (7:1–8), worshiping in a rebuilt temple (11:1–3), and suffering at the hand of the Antichrist.

Not as widely published but at least as widely believed is the *Moderate Futurist* view. This proposes the Book of Revelation as summarizing the conclusion of the church's age-long procession through tribulation and triumph, warfare and victory, and consummating in the climactic return of Jesus Christ for His church. The Tribulation is generally viewed as agelong, but increasing in intensity, so that the church is understood as present through much of the Earth's turmoil until just prior to the outpouring of the "bowls full of the wrath of God" (15:7). This occurs during chapter 16 and culminates in the collapse of the present world order (chs. 17; 18).

Among other views are these: 1) The *Historic* position sees Revelation as a symbolic prophecy of the whole of church history, with the events of the book a picture of the events and movements that have shaped the conflict and progress of the Christian church. 2) The *Preterist* views Revelation as a message of hope and comfort to the first-century believers only, offering them an expectation of their deliverance from Roman persecution and oppression. 3) The *Idealist* formulates no particular historical focus or effort at interpreting specifics of the book, rather seeing it as a broad, poetic portrayal of the conflict between the kingdom of God and the powers of Satan.[1]

THE PRETERIST APPROACH

The preterist approach sees Revelation as a book written primarily for the first-century church. According to this view, everything in the Book of Revelation, with the one exception of the ultimate return of Christ, has already taken place. This view may seem unusual to those who have held a different view and have never heard of this interpretation; however, it is a view held by sincere believers in Christ. As we also stated in reference to the Rapture, we must remember that, particularly in regard to prophecies of the end times, we see through a glass darkly, and topics of such uncertain interpretation should never be a division between believers.

Let us look together at some passages in Revelation and see how they might apply to first-century believers.

Read Revelation 6.

This passage contains the seal judgments. What are the consequences of each of the first five seals?

The first seal has been variously interpreted, but the next four seals are clear in their meaning. Were these types of judgments occurring in the first century? Can you think of any specific examples?

Revelation was probably written within twenty years of the destruction of Jerusalem (A.D. 70). How might the early church have seen that event alluded to in this passage?

The fifth seal refers to believers being martyred for their faith. What references can you find in Revelation 1—3 that indicate that the church of that day was being persecuted?

Read Revelation 13:1–10.

Who is the dragon?

In the first century, who would have been seen as the beast?

Many scholars believe that Revelation was written during the reign of Domitian. At that time emperor worship was mandatory, and Christians were severely persecuted for their refusal to participate. What elements in this passage could be interpreted as being fulfilled in the above-mentioned conditions?

Read Revelation 17 and Zechariah 5:5–11.

What is the woman in Revelation 17 called?

What is another name for the "land of Shinar"? (Zech. 5:11)

What other parallels do you see between these two passages?

Revelation 17:9 refers to seven mountains on which the woman sits. What city is built on seven hills? How do you think first-century believers saw this passage?

In these passages we see some examples of how the preterist interpretation can explain the prophecies of Revelation from the view of the first century, and as applying to the first century. Other parts of Revelation depict the praise and worship going on in heaven. These passages also could easily be tied to the preterist view because the praises of the saints in heaven are always going up before the throne.

THE IDEALIST VIEW

Now let's consider the idealist view. According to this view, the Book of Revelation is a symbolic representation of the spiritual struggle of the church throughout the ages. In this view there are few specific references to actual historic events or people; rather the purpose of the book is to illustrate great spiritual principles or truths that guide the church of all ages. This view is probably best illustrated in Revelation 12.

Read Revelation 12.

Who is the woman?

Who is the dragon?

Who is the male Child?

What event is depicted in verses 7–9?

How could verses 7–11 be interpreted as symbolically representing the agelong struggle? What would be the message conveyed by this interpretation?

What message regarding God's overseeing of His people and His plan is shown in verses 13–17?

Seeing this passage as a general statement of the agelong spiritual warfare that the church is engaged in, we can recognize several important lessons. We see that the ultimate defeat of Satan is already assured. We see that the work of Satan on earth will be intense and will become even more intense as the end nears. And we see that God is able to preserve His people.

Read Revelation 18:1–8. Consider Babylon as being a symbol of the world system, or the characteristic mind-set and value system of this age. Answer the following, keeping in mind that we are considering this passage from the idealist view.

What does verse 2 tell us about the ultimate source of the world system and about its destiny?

What does verse 3 indicate about the scope, or extent of influence, of the world system?

What is the message of verse 4?

To whom are verses 6 and 7 addressed?

What do verses 5–8 say about the judgment of Babylon?

THE HISTORIC INTERPRETATION

The historic system of interpretation sees Revelation as prophetic of all of church history. In this view many of the prophecies can be said to have been fulfilled repeatedly, for the church has repeatedly faced similar trials. Perhaps the best example of this is in Revelation 13:7, which states that the beast will "make war with the saints." This can be seen as being fulfilled many times in periods of persecution that the church has faced. Thus the beast can be said to have been Domitian and Diocletian in Roman times, and Stalin and Mao in modern times.

Read Revelation 17. Using the historic approach to Revelation, what things, systems, or events of the church age could be represented by Babylon?

THE MODERATE FUTURIST VIEW

The moderate futurist system of interpretation also sees Revelation as pertaining to the church throughout the age. But whereas the symbolic view would not see direct fulfillment of these prophecies, and the historic view would see Revelation as continuously being fulfilled in the history of the church, here is the moderate futurist view, which sees many of the judgments as representing agelong forces. (Other aspects of the judgments prophesied would be seen as pertaining to the end of time.) The elements of God's judgment that occur throughout time, have demonstrably increased in their intensity or severity as the end approaches. Jesus noted this in Matthew 24:4–14. Thus, many events that are considered to belong to the Great Tribulation in other systems of prophecy are seen as ongoing judgments through this present age in the moderate futurist system.

Read Revelation 6:1–11.

Is there any indication in this text that these things are confined to a time at the end of the age?

Throughout history do we see these types of events?

How does this text correspond to Matthew 24:4–14? List parallels.

We see immediately that this view does not confine Revelation to an entirely future role. Many events of Revelation are seen as already in motion, and we are seen as active participants in the ongoing final acts of redemptive history leading to the finale.

 PROBING THE DEPTHS

The First Seal. This seal is subject to two opposite interpretations. The typical dispensational interpretation sees the rider of the white horse as being the Antichrist. The rider is given a bow but no arrows; this represents the peaceful, but deceitful, takeover of the world government that will occur under Antichrist.

The other interpretation sees the rider of the horse as Jesus Christ. In this interpretation the first seal signifies Christ's going forth in triumph, leading His church through the agelong struggle to victory, an interpretation very consistent with the ultimate message of Revelation.

The fact that this verse is interpreted in two so totally opposite ways should make us realize that we need to approach this book without dogmatism and with humility. Dedicated scholars differ on this point but unite on the ultimate truth of Revelation: Jesus is Lord and will come as King of kings.

When we reach the sixth seal we see another aspect of the moderate futurist system. This approach does not constrain Revelation to be in chronological sequence, but emphasizes the discursive nature of all prophecy. (The dispensational approach, which we will consider next, does see the majority of Revelation as being basically chronological.) In our studies of the nature of prophecy, we noted that prophecy is discursive in nature. Therefore, the prophets wrote what they saw, but their visions would not be of things which would follow one another in time, but which would either overlap, contain time gaps, or occur in reverse order. Revelation, as a book of prophecy, is no different, and in considering the sixth seal we can see an example of that.

Read Revelation 6:12–17.

List six things that occur in verses 12–14.

What was the response of the people on earth?

Read Revelation 8:5.

What is the context of this verse?

List four things that occur here.

Read Revelation 11:15–19.

What event is the occasion for this outburst of praise in heaven?

List seven things that occur in verse 19.

Read Revelation 16:17–21.

List four things that occur in verse 18.

What occurs in verse 21?

What is the response of the people on earth?

In the four passages we have just considered, what common elements do you see?

Could these passages be referring to the same event?

This view (that the three earthquakes are the same event) is generally held by the Pre-Wrath Rapture interpretation. Since that view does not see a formal seven-year "Great Tribulation" it becomes impossible to pin down a position on the Rapture in terms of "the Tribulation." Rather, the moderate futurist view sees a short period of final, intense judgment wherein *the wrath of God* is poured out on the earth. This is generally seen as comprising the "bowl judgments" of Revelation 16. A time period for those judgments is not always specified, but some think the three and one-half years frequently referenced is a possible duration for this period of God's Wrath.

THE DISPENSATIONAL VIEW

The final view of Revelation that we will discuss is the dispensational view. Dispensationalism is an interpretive system that affects one's view of God's work in the whole Bible. A key feature of this system is the separation of God's work within national Israel from His work within the church. Dispensationalists believe that the promises made to Israel in the Old Testament will be literally fulfilled to national Israel. By this view, the church is seldom, if ever, mentioned in the Old Testament. When Jesus came, a "kingdom offer" was made to the Jewish people; they rejected it. Therefore, God established the church and postponed all the promises to Israel until the end of the age when Israel will again be God's people on earth after the Rapture. This view sees miracles and other Holy Spirit gifts as only occurring in the first century and not today. In prophecy, according to this view, Revelation has very little present import. This is because the dispensationalist sees Revelation 4:1 as the Rapture; and because the church is not on earth while the judgments in Revelation take place, it has little relevance to the church today. However, Revelation is seen as allowing us to see the working out of God's plan for Israel, and helping us to see the signs of Christ's return. Let us examine some of the key passages in the dispensational interpretation of Revelation.

Read Revelation 1:19 and 4:1.

What three categories of things is John commanded to write?

Who commanded John to write?

What did John see in 4:1?

What command did he receive?

When were the things that John saw going to take place?

These two verses are key in the dispensational approach to Revelation. Revelation 1:19 is a basic outline of the book. Dispensationalists say that the "things which you have seen" refers to John's vision of the glorified Christ (Rev. 1). "The things which are" encompass the letters to the seven churches (Rev. 2; 3). And the "things which will take place after this" refers to prophecies of the end times which comprise everything from Revelation 4:1 through the end of the book. Revelation 4:1 is, therefore, a turning point in the book; it is also a prophecy of the Rapture according to the dispensational view. The command, "Come up here," is seen as being symbolic of the Rapture of the church.

From 4:1 on, the events related in Revelation are future and also largely chronological. Thus, the seal judgments begin the Great Tribulation, and the seventh seal initiates the trumpet judgments, and so on. Let us examine some results of this view.

Read Revelation 6:9–11.

According to the dispensational view, is this before or after the Rapture?

Who are these martyrs? Where do these believers come from?

In the dispensational view the forces of the world government are gathered against national Israel at the end of the Tribulation. It is their goal to destroy Israel, but Jesus will return with His saints and destroy the opposing forces in the battle of Armageddon. He then will set up a 1,000-year reign during which the prophetic promises to Israel are all fulfilled. In the following texts, tell how this position is supported:

Rev. 16:12–16

Rev. 19:17–21

Rev. 20:4–6

Finally, the dispensational view, as stated above, is always premillennial. That is, supporters of this view believe that Jesus will return prior to the Millennium, and that He will reign on earth for a thousand years. There are other views that are premillennial but not dispensational, and there are views that are not premillennial at all. But the details of beliefs about the Millennium will be covered in a future lesson.

 FAITH ALIVE

We must keep foremost in our minds that the ultimate triumph of Jesus Christ over all the economic, political, and spiritual forces that currently strive over the earth is the message of the Book of Revelation. With that in mind, praise the Lord for His ultimate victory. With His victory in mind, what trials are you facing that you can trust Him for victory over?

1. *Spirit-Filled Life Bible* (Nashville, TN: Thomas Nelson Publishers, 1991), 1966, "Kingdom Dynamics: Interpretive Approaches to the Book of Revelation."

Lesson 9/Interpretations of Daniel

Several of the most well-known stories in the Bible are found in the Book of Daniel. From childhood we are told of Daniel in the lions' den, the three Hebrew children in the fiery furnace, the handwriting on the wall, and other stories from this remarkable book. Indeed, the adventures of Daniel and his friends are among the most vivid and dramatic in Scripture. But Daniel is also, undoubtedly, the most significant Old Testament book regarding end times prophecy, and we cannot overlook the Book of Daniel in our study.

In this lesson we will examine some key prophecies in Daniel, and we will see where parallels exist between Daniel, the Olivet Discourse, and Revelation. But let us begin by finding out something about Daniel himself.

 BEHIND THE SCENES

Daniel was a young man, probably in his early teens, when he was deported to Babylon in 605 B.C. At this time, Nebuchadnezzar took the upper echelon of the Jewish society into captivity, leaving only the poorest of the land (2 Kin. 24:14). This indicates that Daniel was from an elite family; he may have been related to the king.

Daniel was recognized for his wisdom and knowledge; he was among the young men who were chosen to serve in the palace of Nebuchadnezzar. His wisdom and insight enabled him to rise to the highest levels of Nebuchadnezzar's court, and his integrity and righteousness became an example to the Jewish exiles.

Daniel is a prime example of loyalty. His unswerving loyalty to the kings he served made him a highly valued and trusted advisor. But above that, his first loyalty was to God. Daniel showed uncompromising courage in his loyalty to God, and his trust in God enabled him to face any consequences with assurance of ultimate victory.

Read Daniel 2. This text tells of a time when God miraculously revealed to Daniel the dream of Nebuchadnezzar. By this revelation, God spared the lives of Daniel and others; He also gave Daniel a broad outline of history from that day unto the end of the age. Let us quickly review some ancient history before we consider this dream.

 BEHIND THE SCENES

Around 1000 B.C. David was reigning over a united Israel. His son, Solomon, would reign over Israel's Golden Age, at which time Israel reached the zenith of its political power and influence. But at this same time, the Assyrian Empire was beginning to take shape in Mesopotamia. The strength of Assyria grew until, in 671 B.C., they defeated Egypt and established control over all of the ancient Near East. (In the course of their conquests, they destroyed Samaria and took the northern kingdom of Israel into captivity.)

However, their dominion was short-lived. Less than sixty years later, the Babylonians, in alliance with the Medes, destroyed Nineveh, the capital of Assyria, breaking the power of the Assyrian Empire. Soon after, in 605 B.C., the Babylonians defeated the Egyptians at Carchemish, and the Babylonian rulership was established.

After being under Babylonian rule for a time, Judah revolted and was attacked by Nebuchadnezzar. In 586 B.C. Jerusalem was destroyed, and Judah ceased to exist as a kingdom.

The Babylonian Empire fared no better than the Assyrian, for only sixty-six years after their victory at Carchemish, Babylon fell to the Medes and the Persians. The Persians took control of the Empire in 539 B.C.

As we saw in lesson 2, the rise of Alexander the Great marked the fall of the Persian Empire. From 334 B.C. to

326 B.C. Alexander was unstoppable. He conquered all of the Persian Empire and more. After Alexander's death in 323 B.C., his empire was divided among four of his generals. These four kingdoms were called the Hellenistic Monarchies, and, in typical human fashion, they warred among themselves, eventually allowing Rome to conquer all.

The Roman Republic was beginning to develop in Italy even before the time of Alexander the Great. But it was under Julius Caesar that world dominance became a reality. Between 58 B.C. and 45 B.C. Julius Caesar established the control of Rome from Britain to Egypt. The Roman Empire was to last for hundreds of years, and it dwarfed all its predecessors in longevity and in influence.

Look again at Daniel 2:31–45. What did the four types of metal represent?

What four kingdoms are represented here?

What represented God's kingdom?

What will be the duration of God's kingdom?

This dream and interpretation provide a good starting point for our study of Daniel, for it allows us to see the basic frame of reference that Daniel had. In other visions which Daniel had, we will repeatedly see those same four kingdoms.

Before we leave our consideration of Nebuchadnezzar's dream, we must consider the feet "partly of iron and partly of clay." In various systems of prophecy, the ten toes are identified as ten kings or kingdoms which will arise out of the Roman Empire in the last days. Later in Daniel, and also in Revelation, we see parallels of these ten kings.

Read Daniel 7:7–12 and Revelation 13:1, 2.

What do the ten horns in Daniel chapter 7 represent? (see verse 24)

In either Daniel 2 or in Revelation 13, is it explicitly indicated what the toes or horns represent?

Seeing that the number ten is frequently thought to symbolize human government, what other interpretation or significance could be given to these symbols?

This speculation on alternative interpretations is not meant to imply that the idea of ten kingdoms is wrong. Indeed, we are told in Daniel 7 that the horns are ten kings, and there is every reason to believe that John saw the same beast in Revelation 13. Therefore, the horns in Revelation 13 would also represent the ten kings. However, keeping in mind the fact of multiple fulfillment of prophecy, we are not out of line in examining other possible interpretations of that vision.

Let us consider Daniel's visions of the beasts in chapter 7 and chapter 8 more closely. These visions relate to a great span of history, and you may wish to review the overview of ancient history earlier in the lesson.

Read Daniel 7 and 8.

In Daniel 7, what empires are represented by the various animals?

How does this correspond with Daniel 2?

In Daniel 8, what empires are represented?

What elements in the visions in chapters 7 and 8 support your choice for the representation of Greece?

Do the little horn in chapter 7 and the little horn in chapter 8 represent the same thing?

There is some difference of opinion about the empires represented in chapter 7. On one hand, some see the four empires in chapter 7 as parallels to the empires in chapter 2. Further support is given to this view by the parallels we saw between the fourth beast in Daniel 7 and the beast of Revelation (which many see as an extension of the Roman Empire). On the other hand, some see the four beasts of chapter 7 as representing Babylon, Media, Persia, and Greece. Their primary support lies in equating the little horn in chapter 7 with the little horn in chapter 8. The little horn in chapter 8 rises out of the Grecian Empire, so if it be identical with the little horn of chapter 7, then the fourth beast in chapter 7 must be Greece. According to this view, the little horn is identified as Antiochus Epiphanes, although it may also represent the Antichrist.

 ### BEHIND THE SCENES

During the intertestamental period, the Greek Empire was established in the Near East and ruled over Judea. When the Greek Empire was divided, the rulership of Judea came under the Seleucid monarchs. One of these kings, Antiochus Epiphanes, is often identified with the little horn in Daniel 7 and 8, as well as the "one who makes desolate" (Dan. 9:27). This ruler bitterly oppressed the religious Jews, forbidding the practice of circumcision, and even offering pagan sacrifices in the temple. Judas ben Mattathias (*Makkabaios* in Greek, from which we get "Maccabees") and his sons began a revolt, which eventually resulted in the withdrawing of the anti-Jewish decrees and the reestablishing of the temple worship. The Feast of Hanukkah celebrates the rededication of the temple at this time, after it had been cleansed from the pagan worship that had gone on under Antiochus Epiphanes.[1]

With the varying interpretations of these chapters, it is easy to get lost in the details of how the visions fit into one's system of prophecy. However, we must not lose sight of the overriding message to God's people: *Through this present age there will be a struggle with evil, but the kingdom of God will be established and His rule will be forever!*

 ## PROBING THE DEPTHS

Daniel's prophecy in chapter 7 not only spans the spiritual struggle covering the ages through Messiah's First and Second Coming, but it uses two terms important to perceiving the biblical truth of the kingdom of God: "dominion" and "possess." "Dominion" (from Chaldee, *shelet,* "to govern, prevail, dominate") is in the hands of world powers (vv. 6, 12) until the Coming of the Son of Man, at which time it is taken by Him forever (vv. 13, 14). But an interim struggle is seen between the First and Second Coming of Messiah.

During this season, the saints "possess" (Chaldee, *chacan,* "to hold on or occupy") the kingdom. This communicates a process of long struggle as the redeemed ("saints") "possess" what they have "received" (v. 18). The scenario reads: 1) After the "judgment was made *in favor of* the saints" (v. 22—a forecast of the pivotal impact of Christ's Cross upon which hinged both man's redemption as well as his reinstatement to the potential of his rule under God), an extended struggle ensues. 2) This struggle is described as the "time [which] came for the saints to possess the kingdom." They do battle against sinister adversaries and experience a mix of victories and apparent defeats (v. 25).

The prophecy unveils the present age of the kingdom, which is one of ongoing struggle—with victory upon victory for the church. Yet it withholds its conclusive triumph until Christ comes again.

This prophecy also balances the question of divine sovereignty and human responsibility. 1) God's sovereignty accomplishes the foundational victory (v. 22) and in the Cross achieves the decisive victory, allowing the saints new dimensions for advance and conquest. 2) He entrusts the responsibility for that advance to His own to "possess the kingdom," entering into conflict with the Adversary, at times at the expense of their apparent defeat (v. 25). 3) However, movement toward victory is theirs as they press the "judgment" of the "court" (vv. 22, 26) and seize realms controlled by evil. They wrestle the dominion from hellish powers, continuing in warfare until the ultimate seating of the Son of Man (vv. 14, 27).

Prophetic systems vary as to how and when these words unfold on the calendar of church history, for the passage is subject to different schemes of interpretation, each with different projected chronologies. But the foundational fact remains that an agelong struggle between "the saints" and the power of evil in the world calls each believer to a commitment to steadfast battle, a mixture of victories with setbacks, and a consummate triumph anticipated at Christ's Coming. In the meantime, we "receive" the kingdom and pursue victories for our King, by His power, making intermittent gains—all of which are based on "the judgment" achieved through the Cross. See Revelation 12:10, 11.[2]

DANIEL'S SEVENTY WEEKS

In Daniel 9 we have one of the crucial prophecies in the Bible: the Seventy Weeks prophecy. As we have seen with other prophecies throughout Daniel, there are primarily two schools of thought regarding this prophecy. The Classical approach sees the numbers in this passage as being symbolic and the initial fulfillment of this prophecy being at the time of Antiochus Epiphanes. Subsequent fulfillments may also be seen in Jesus and the destruction of the temple, and also possibly in the end times.

The Dispensational viewpoint sees the numbers as literal and sees a great time gap (the church age) between the sixty-ninth and seventieth weeks. The seventieth week will be the seven years of the Great Tribulation. Let's examine this prophecy and the two interpretations.

Read Daniel 9.

What caused Daniel to intercede for Jerusalem and the people?

A great principle of intercessory prayer is illustrated by Daniel: he identifies with the people and with the sin of the people. How many times does Daniel say "we" or "us" in his prayer?

According to verse 24, what six goals are to be accomplished in the seventy weeks?

In verses 25 and 26 Messiah is mentioned. What does "messiah" mean?

From that meaning could the title apply to others than Christ?

In verse 26, who are possible candidates for "the prince who is to come"?

In verse 27, who is "he"?

According to the classical interpretation, the 490 years represent a lifetime (70 years) seven times over. Seven represents completion, so it is as though the Lord were saying to Daniel, "You have prayed regarding this seventy-year prophecy, but I tell you that there is to be a full completion of judgment before all of My goals are accomplished." Thus, the numbers could be considered symbolic.

Such an interpretation also sees multiple fulfillment of prophecy in this passage; the initial fulfillment taking place during the Second Century B.C. when Antiochus Epiphanes oppressed the Jews. The messiah spoken of ("messiah" meaning "anointed one") was the High Priest Onias III, and the oppression of Jerusalem and desecration of the temple are what is referred to in 9:27. The consummation is the revolt of the Jews and the restoration of the temple worship.

Another view sees fulfillment as being in the time of Christ. In this case Jesus is the Messiah who is cut off for our sins. The "people of the prince who is to come" refers to the Roman destruction of Jerusalem under Titus in A.D. 70, and "he" (v. 27) refers back to Jesus; His covenant is confirmed with all of God's people, both Old and New Testament believers. In the middle of the full time of God's redemptive work, He brought an end to sacrifice by offering Himself.

Finally, the classical approach sees that there could yet even be another fulfillment in the end times.

By comparison, the dispensational interpretation of this passage sees a literal "69 weeks" (483 years) from the decree of Artaxerxes to rebuild Jerusalem in 445 B.C. to Jesus' death in A.D. 32. The end of verse 26 is believed to refer to Titus's destruction of Jerusalem, but between the sixty-ninth and seventieth weeks the dispensationalist sees a great hiatus of the church age—the undefined term of the present era until the Rapture. In the dispensationalist's eyes, the church was not seen nor prophesied at all in the Old Testament, for that aspect of God's plan was not determined until the Jews of Jesus' day rejected the "kingdom offer." Thus, Daniel's final "seventieth week" is seen as yet in the future and to be fulfilled in the seven years of the Great Tribulation.

By this interpretation, "he" in verse 27 refers to the Antichrist and his dealings with the Jews during the Great Tribulation. The concept of a seven-year Great Tribulation is directly connected to this passage. There are many references to three and one-half years, but only this one mention of a seven-year period.

There are many significant allusions to Daniel's Seventy Weeks prophecy both in the Olivet Discourse and in Revelation. In Matthew 24:15 Jesus refers directly to the "'abomination of desolation,' spoken of by Daniel the prophet." According to the dispensational view, this refers to a future desecration of the temple by the Antichrist. In this interpretation, at the beginning of the Tribulation the Antichrist will enter a covenant with Israel, which will allow sacrificial worship to be resumed. After three and one-half years ("in the middle of the week," Dan. 9:27) he will stop the sacrifices and desecrate the temple by setting up an image of himself and requiring worship. Let us examine the references that are cited in support of this scenario.

Read Daniel 9:27; Matthew 24:15; 2 Thessalonians 2:3, 4; and Revelation 13.

What references and terms in these passages possibly refer to the temple or temple worship?

What references speak of an image?

What references may be speaking of an image being erected in the temple?

What time references are given in Daniel? How do they correlate with the time reference in Revelation 13:5?

We have seen that the context of the Matthew passage supports a Post-Tribulation Rapture view (lesson 7). What view (if any) is supported by these other passages?

Chapters 10—12 of Daniel record the final vision and prophecy of this book. After a time of fasting and prayer, Daniel has a vision of a heavenly messenger. This messenger gives Daniel a prophetic message relating to kings of the North and South. As we have seen in many of Daniel's prophecies, the fulfillment can be seen in events of the intertestamental period as well as in events of the end times.

Read Daniel 11. Who is the "mighty king" in verse 3?

In this passage the king of the South is seen as Egypt under the Ptolemys, and the king of the North is Seleucid Syria. Much of the chapter relates to ongoing conflict which was incessant among the Hellenistic Monarchies. Portions of the chapter may refer to various kings of Egypt and Syria, including Ptolemy III, Antiochus III, Ptolemy V, and Antiochus IV (Epiphanes).

Daniel 11:29–35 is among the portions of this chapter believed to refer to Antiochus Epiphanes. What parallels do you see with other prophecies in Daniel?

What things will the king in verse 36 do?

Compare that verse with Revelation 13:5 and 6. List similarities.

Who is this king?

This portion may be speaking of Antiochus or Antichrist. Of course, a reference to Antiochus would not negate the possibility that a further fulfillment is yet to occur.

Read Daniel 12:1–3. Compare verse 1 with Revelation 12:7–9. Comment on the relationship between these passages.

The "time of trouble" in Daniel 12:1 would refer to what in dispensational interpretation?

Consider the statement, "Your people shall be delivered, every one who is found written in the book" (v. 1). Who are "your people"? (Compare Rev. 20:15.)

To what does Daniel 12:2 refer?

Here, at the end of Daniel's prophecies, we see direct parallels to the end of Revelation: the resurrection and final judgment. With that promise of judgment comes a promise of blessing for the righteous as well. For after that judgment "the righteous will shine forth as the sun in the kingdom of their Father" (Matt. 13:43).

FAITH ALIVE

Consider how Daniel prophesies so much about history, and about so much that has been fulfilled. Does that reinforce your belief in God's control of history and human affairs?

How does it make you feel about the prophecies yet to be fulfilled?

Praise God for His sovereignty and for His oversight of history. Thank Him that He is not too big to be concerned about your personal history.

1. Douglas, J. D., ed., *New Bible Dictionary* (Grand Rapids, MI: Wm. B. Eerdmans Publishing Co., 1962), 762–764, "Maccabees."

2. *Spirit-Filled Life Bible* (Nashville, TN: Thomas Nelson Publishers, 1991), 1244, 1245, "Kingdom Dynamics: Old Testament: Possessing the Kingdom."

Lesson 10/Views of the Millennium

In these past lessons we have examined events leading up to the return of Christ. We now look beyond His return to the time when Christ's rulership is established. But is that rulership established for eternity at that time, or is there a final stage in God's redemptive plan for earth? This question is central to the study of the Millennium.

WHAT IS THE MILLENNIUM?

The Millennium is a term usually referring to a one thousand-year period following the Second Coming wherein Christ and His saints reign over the earth. The primary biblical support for this doctrine comes from Revelation 20.

Read Revelation 20:1–6.

What happens to Satan in this passage?

Why is Satan bound?

Who reigns with Christ?

How long is this reign?

How many times does this passage mention one thousand years?

It would seem that this passage is straightforward enough that there would be general agreement about the Millennium. However, there are a number of different views about how this passage ought to be interpreted and about how these things are accomplished in history. We will look at four views of the Millennium: the premillennial, dispensational, postmillennial, and amillennial. These views can be grouped into two pairs. The premillennial and dispensational views believe that the return of Christ will usher in the Millennium, whereas the postmillennial and amillennial views see Christ's coming as initiating the eternal age to come.

THE POSTMILLENNIAL VIEW

One approach to this view was popular about one hundred years ago among liberal Protestants. Their idea was that the Christian community would gradually transform society through its moral guidance. This would result in an extended period of peace and harmony on earth; after which the Lord Jesus would return to receive the kingdom established on earth by the church. The "progress" of history in the twentieth century has dampened enthusiasm for this version of postmillennialism, but it still has adherents today.

Another version of postmillennialism that has an evangelical following today sees the Millennium not as a "golden age" in the history of man but as the reign of Christ being realized wherever the kingdom of God is received. Thus, the kingdom is a spiritual reality achieved through the ministry of the church rather than a political reality achieved through Christians' social activism.

THE AMILLENNIAL VIEW

The amillennial view is similar to the postmillennial view in that it sees the Second Coming as a single event that brings about the final judgment and the opening of the age to come. Unlike the postmillennial view, the amillennial view sees the thousand-year reign of Jesus prophesied in Revelation 20 as being entirely symbolic.

The basic arguments against premillennialism (by supporters of the amillennial or postmillennial views) relate to their entire approach to eschatology, that is, to the doctrine of "last things." These note that from the time of the early church, and throughout history, Christians have believed that Jesus was coming again, the resurrection would occur, and Christ would judge mankind. (See examples of credal statements in lesson 6.) Consider the following texts, which refer to the end of time.

Read Matthew 25:31–46.

What event is this text talking about?

According to verse 31, when does this occur?

Who is judged?

What is the end result of this judgment?

Is there any indication of more than one resurrection or judgment?

Read John 5:24–30.

Who will execute judgment?

Who will not come into judgment?

What two groups will be raised?

What are the destinies of those who are raised?

Is there any indication of more than one resurrection or judgment?

Read 2 Timothy 4:1.

When will the Lord Jesus Christ judge?

Who will the Lord Jesus Christ judge?

Does this text imply one resurrection?

In light of these and similar passages, opponents of premillennialism argue that there is one Second Coming that is concomitant to the resurrection and judgment. Obviously, if these three events are inseparably connected and unified, there is no place to insert a thousand-year earthly reign of Christ. Seen from this theological perspective, Revelation 20 must be viewed as symbolic or as applying to the agelong spiritual activity of the church.

THE DISPENSATIONAL VIEW

The dispensational view is premillennial, but it is significantly different from older premillennialism. In *Wrongly Dividing the Word of Truth,* Dr. John Gerstner lists ten distinguishing features of dispensational premillennialism versus the older premillennial view.

1. Older premillennialism taught that the church was in the forevision of the Old Testament prophecy; dispensationalism teaches that the church is hardly, if at all, in the Old Testament Prophets.

2. Older premillennialism taught that the great burden of Old Testament prophecy was the coming of Christ to die (at the First Advent) and the kingdom age (at the Second Advent). Dispensationalism says that the great burden of Old Testament prophecy is the kingdom of the Jews.

3. Older premillennialism taught that the First Advent was the specific time for Christ to die for man's sin; Dispensationalism teaches that the kingdom (earthly) should have been set up at the First Advent for that was the predicted time of its coming.

4. Older premillennialism taught that the present age of grace was designed by God and predicted in the Old Testament; Dispensationalism holds that the present age was unforeseen in the Old Testament and thus is a "great parenthesis" introduced because the Jews rejected the kingdom.

5. Older premillennialism taught that one may divide time in any way desirable so long as one allows for a millennium after the Second Advent; Dispensationalism maintains that the only allowable way to divide time is in seven dispensations. The present age is the sixth such dispensation; the last one will be the millennial age after the Second Advent. It is from this division of time that Dispensationalism gets its name.

6. Older premillennialism taught that the Second Advent was to be one event; Dispensationalism holds that the Second Advent will be in two sections—"the Rapture" and "the Revelation." Between these two events they put the (to them) unfulfilled seventieth week (seven years) of Daniel 9:23–27, which they call "the Great Tribulation."

7. Older premillennialism taught that certain signs must precede the Second Advent; Dispensationalism teaches that no sign precedes the "rapture-stage" of the Second Advent. The "Rapture" could occur "at any moment," but the "Revelation" must take place after the seven years of the Great Tribulation. The first stage is undated and unannounced; the second stage is dated and announced.

8. Older premillennialism had two resurrections—the righteous before the Millennium; the unrighteous after the Millennium. Dispensationalism has introduced a third resurrection—"tribulation-saints" at the "revelation-stage" of the Second Advent.

9. Older premillennialism usually held what is called the "historical-symbolic" view of the book of Revelation. This view makes Revelation a picture in symbolic form of the main events in the present age. Dispensationalism holds generally to the "futurist" view of the book of Revelation, which view makes almost the whole book (especially chapters 4 to 19) a literal description of events to take place during "the Great Tribulation" of Daniel's seventieth week, which Dispensationalism considers as yet unfulfilled.

10. The general attitude of older premillennialism was on the whole mild and reverent in its approach to Scripture. There have been some outstanding scholars who have been persuaded that the premillennial is the correct view. In contrast, Dispensationalism has assumed a far more dogmatic attitude. It has introduced a number of novelties in prophetic interpretation that the church never heard of until about a century ago.[1]

Irrespective of one's prophetic or biblical approach in interpretation, we see that the dispensational interpretation of the Millennium is determined by a theological perspective rather than by overwhelming biblical evidence. However, we must realize that this is no less true of others. *All* millennial views are conditioned by the theology of their proponents. Those who do not believe in a literal Millennium believe that the biblical evidence for Christ's Second Coming being immediately followed by the judgment outweighs the need to interpret Revelation 20 literally. Those who interpret Revelation 20 literally (i.e., an exact 1,000 years), conform other aspects of their theology and biblical interpretation to allow this. In no single view is the case so airtight as to be irrefutable. We must recognize this fact and be charitable to believers holding other views on this doctrine. Perhaps nothing would be so unwise as to part fellowship on these points. Devoted believers embrace each view, and we would be wise to simply accept our view and be humble enough to deny our own omniscience.

As mentioned above, several distinguishing points between dispensational premillennialism and older premillennialism relate to Old Testament interpretation. The Old Testament prophets regularly spoke of a future time when the Lord would rule from Jerusalem and Israel would be dominant among the nations. From the dispensational viewpoint, these prophecies relate literally to national Israel.

Read Zephaniah 3:14–20. To whom is this passage directed?

What titles are given to God's people?

What titles are given to God?

What statements indicate deliverance and dominance for Israel?

What other blessings are promised?

In this passage we see blessings of deliverance from judgment, peace, and exaltation given to Israel. In no place is there any indication that the Gentiles will be included. The dispensational view interprets this very literally: the promises were given to Israel, and they shall be fulfilled to Israel! Therefore, the dispensational theology needs a time period wherein these promises can be fulfilled to Israel; a time in which the church (the other people of God) is not on earth. They see the Millennium as being this time. The church is raptured prior to the Great Tribulation. Seven years later, the Lord returns to set up an earthly kingdom in which national Israel is dominant. During that reign, all the prophecies are fulfilled which speak of Israel's rulership and the future "golden age" of Israel.

THE PREMILLENNIAL VIEW

One commentator representing this view has summarized it this way:

The biblical Millennium will be a period of peace, love, and brotherhood when all nature lives in the harmony that was intended in the Garden of Eden. The Book of Isaiah (11:6–9) speaks of a time when the wild animals will live at peace with domestic animals, when the serpents will no longer bite. A little child will be able to play by a cobra's den or lead wild beasts around and not be harmed. Military schools will close, and implements of war will no longer be manufactured. The money and resources that now go into warfare will then be devoted to peaceful pursuits. When this day comes, every person will have his own plot of ground, his own home. All will live in harmony with their neighbors. No one will be afraid that someone will try to steal his belongings. There will be universal peace, for the knowledge of the Lord will cover the Earth as the waters cover the sea.

I believe the Millennium is a transition period, when Jesus Christ comes back to Earth to show mankind what it would have been like if sin had never entered the world. It will be a time when Jesus Christ will reign as king, and the kingdom of God will be established on Earth. There will be a one-world government under the leadership of Jesus with nation-states subject to Him. The Bible says that representatives of the nations of the Earth will come to Jerusalem each year (Is. 2:2–4; Zech. 14:16).[2]

This view of the Millennium is commonly held by non-dispensational premillennialists. The idea of an Edenic restoration, where all creation is in a state of peace and harmony, is a commonly held notion, and the passage in Isaiah 11 mentioned above is one of the most quoted texts. Let's look at that text.

Read Isaiah 11:1–11.

Of whom is this passage speaking?

What type of conditions are illustrated in verses 6–8?

What brings about those conditions?

What two groups of people are referred to in verses 10 and 11?

Premillennialists say that this passage refers to the Millennium. By what line of reasoning can that view be supported?

Again we see that, to some extent, the Millennium must be read into this passage rather than extracted from it. Many scholars contend that this passage refers to the First Coming of Christ and the peace that Christ brought to groups that were formerly hostile to one another. Let us examine one additional passage regarding the Millennium.

Read Micah 4:1–5. What elements in this passage correspond with the description of the Millennium with which we began our study of the premillennial view?

Look again at the basic text for the Millennium (Rev. 20:1–6). Which features of the Millennium are explicitly stated in Revelation 20?

Micah 4:2 refers to many nations coming to Jerusalem. Does this occur during the Millennium, or might it be speaking of the New Jerusalem in heaven? Give reasons for your answer.

Read the following definition of the word "ever" used in verse 5.

WORD WEALTH

Ever, *'ad.* Everlastingness, perpetuity, eternity, evermore, forever; time passing on and on; world without end; for all time forward; continually. This noun appears nearly fifty times in the Old Testament. Its first occurrence is in Exodus 15:18: "The LORD shall reign forever and ever" (compare Ps. 10:16; Is. 45:17). God dwells eternally in Zion (Ps. 132:14). God inhabits "eternity" (Is. 57:15). In Micah 4:5 Israel vows that they will own Him as their God *Le'Olam Ve'Ad,* forever and ever. In Psalm 132:11, 12, *'ad* describes the length of time that the throne of David shall be occupied by his royal seed: "forevermore." In Isaiah 9:6, Messiah is called "Everlasting Father," which is in Hebrew, *'Abi-'Ad,* literally "Father of Eternity," that is, the architect, builder, begetter, producer, and creator of the ages to come.[3]

How does this affect your interpretation of this passage?

Micah 4:5 is commonly believed to be about the Millennium; however, a good case can also be made for its referring to heaven or the age to come. This is particularly true noting that verse 5 states that "we will walk in the name of the LORD our God forever and ever." Interpreting this passage as being millennial, one would say that the passage refers to the thousand-year reign, but believers do indeed walk in the name of the Lord forever. On the other hand, the amillennialist would say that the statement "forever and ever" refers to the conditions described, not only to the perseverance of believers.

We see again that the theology one brings to a passage will inevitably color his reading of it. When the topic of study is eschatology, this background factor is compounded because there is so much in eschatology that permits various interpretations. In these discussions of eschatology in general and the Millennium in particular it would be good to keep in mind the statement made by George Eldon Ladd when he was discussing the Millennium:

It is unfortunate that the discussion has often been attended by more heat than light. Some expositors insist that any teaching of a reign of Christ on earth before The Age to Come is Jewish rather than Christian doctrine, while others insist that any non-millenarian eschatology is a departure from loyalty to the Word of God. Such reactions are unfortunate. This question, like others which are, from a practical standpoint, far more important, such as that of the subjects for baptism, should be discussed within the household of faith in a spirit of Christian liberty and charity.[4]

 FAITH ALIVE

What have you learned that is new to you?

Can you think of any time when you had trouble understanding another believer because he was speaking from a different view of eschatology?

Does seeing how one's theology colors his interpretation of Scripture make you want to understand more clearly what you yourself believe?

1. *Wrongly Dividing the Word of Truth,* by John H. Gerstner. Copyright © 1991. Word, Inc., Dallas, TX, 18–20. Used with permission.
2. *Spirit-Filled Life Bible* (Nashville, TN: Thomas Nelson Publishers, 1991), 2001, 2002, "Spiritual Answers to Hard Questions: 13. What is the Millennium?"
3. Ibid., 1323, "Word Wealth: 4:5 ever."
4. Ladd, George Eldon, *The Gospel of the Kingdom* (Grand Rapids, MI: Wm. B. Eerdmans Publishing Co., 1959), 35.

Lesson 11/The Final Judgments

After your death you are ushered into a gigantic court-room. Thousands of people are there—waiting to see your judgment. You wait in trepidation. Suddenly, off to your right, a huge movie screen lights up and begins to show your entire life. All of the thoughts, motives, and actions of which you are most ashamed shine forth before the assembled crowd. . . .

This is the idea that many have of the final judgment. But the fact is that the main question will not be, "What did you do in life?" Rather you will answer for what you did with Jesus.

As we have discussed in past lessons, believers in Jesus share the conviction and joyous expectation that Christ will return to earth not only as King, but as Judge, also. This has been a basic tenet of Christianity since the birth of the church. While there is not agreement on the exact relationship in the timing of Christ's return and the judgment, the truth is fully embraced nonetheless. The different views as to how the final judgment will occur are not nearly as varied as views on other aspects of prophecy because most questions of prophetic timing are "past" by the time of the judgment. In this lesson we will consider various aspects of the final judgments, including the different judgments the Bible speaks of, the scope of those judgments, the intermediate state, and the result of the judgments.

THE NUMBER OF JUDGMENTS

The Bible speaks of judgment in many different ways and in reference to different judgments. In the following verses note the subject of judgment and who is judging.

Is. 3:14

John 16:7, 8

1 Cor. 6:2

1 Cor. 6:3

Heb. 10:30

Jude 14, 15

Rev. 18:8

We see that judgment is spoken of diversely and in reference to different types of judgments with different subjects judging and being judged. Additionally, God's judgment is seen at least three different ways: (1) as a present reality, (2) as a final outpouring of wrath on the earth, and (3) as a final assignment of created beings to their eternal destinies. Read the following passages and state which of the three categories of God's judgment the text is speaking of.

Dan. 7:10

Luke 11:31, 32

John 12:31

2 Pet. 2:3

2 Pet. 3:7

Rev. 14:7

When we speak of the final judgments we are referring to that final assignment of created beings to their eternal destinies, but even here we find multiple judgments. The Bible teaches of three different judgments, but each is with a different group and there are distinct differences in consequence.

 AT A GLANCE

TEXT	JUDGMENT	BEING JUDGED	CONSEQUENCE
Rev. 20	White Throne	The Unsaved	Eternal Loss
2 Cor. 5	Christ's "Bema Seat"	The Redeemed	Personal Reward
2 Pet. 2	Angels' Judgment	The Fallen	Eternal Loss

First of all, the Bible speaks of a general judgment. At this stage the wicked and the righteous are separated, and the wicked are sent to eternal condemnation and death. This judgment is called the Great White Throne Judgment in reference to John's vision recorded in Revelation 20.

Read Revelation 20:11–15.

Who is judged in this passage?

Who is the Judge?

By what standard was judgment declared?

Who was cast into the lake of fire?

Read Matthew 25:31–46.

Who is judged in this passage?

Who is the Judge?

By what standards was judgment declared?

What was the destiny of the righteous? of the wicked?

Are these two texts speaking of the same judgment?

In this Great White Throne Judgment, unbelievers are judged "according to their works" (Rev. 20:12). But as believers, we need not fear the judgment, for we who have our names written in the Book of Life have been redeemed by the precious blood of Jesus Christ our Savior.

A second judgment implied in Scripture is the judgment of believers by Jesus Christ. Some people do not distinguish between the general judgment and the judgment of the church; however, there are good scriptural reasons to do so. The Bible speaks quite directly to believers about being judged. But this judgment is not to determine one's eternal destiny; rather it will determine reward.

Read Romans 14:10–12.

Where does this judgment take place?

To whom does this judgment apply?

Who is judging?

On what basis are we judged?

Read 2 Corinthians 5:9–11.

Where does this judgment take place?

Who is being judged?

Who is judging?

On what basis are we judged?

This judgment is sometimes called the Bema Seat Judgment because *bema* is the Greek word translated "judgment seat." This judgment seat is a different setting than the Great White Throne we observe at the general judgment. While it is partly on the basis of the word *bema* being used that this is seen as separate from the general judgment, the primary difference is the fact that the texts involved speak of this event as a more intimate confrontation. The *Bema* judgment is

(1) between Jesus and His church, (2) not related to one's eternal salvation, which is already secured, and (3) regarding one's service to the Lord as His follower/servant; it is deterministic of his or her reward—not eternal state.

WORD WEALTH

Judgment seat, *bema.* From *baino,* "to go," the word described a step or a stride (Acts 7:5). Then it was used for a raised platform reached by steps, especially from which orations were made. Later it denoted the tribune or tribunal of a ruler where litigants stood trial. In the New Testament it mostly refers to earthly magistrates (Acts 18:12, 16, 17), but twice is used of the divine tribunal before which believers will stand (Rom. 14:10; 2 Cor. 5:10).[1]

The other chief passage that concerns the judgment of believers by Christ is in 1 Corinthians.

Read 1 Corinthians 3:10–15.

What will declare or reveal the quality of one's work?

In light of our previous studies, what does "the Day" refer to? (v. 13)

What happens if one's work endures?

What happens if one's work is consumed?

What evidence indicates that this passage is referring to believers?

This passage clearly states that this judgment is not to determine eternal destiny. Rather, the life and works of the

Christian believer are tested, and he is rewarded accordingly. Given the context of the passage, some have said that Paul was speaking about the work of the ministry. However, this does not seem to be supported by the whole of God's Word. Other texts clearly state that each of us should do all we do "in the name of the Lord Jesus" (Col. 3:17). He also speaks of servants working for their earthly masters "with goodwill doing service, as to the Lord, and not to men" (Eph. 6:7). The Word of God does not distinguish between clergy and laity in terms of our primary accountability as His children. Our work, done unto Him and in His will, is judged along with our thoughts, attitudes, and motives. This judgment is Christ's judgment of *believers*, not just of those in the church's leadership. (Church leaders *do* have a distinct accounting, but not at a separate judgment.)

Third, the Bible states that angels will also be judged. In 2 Peter 2:4 we read that the angels who sinned are "reserved for judgment." This tells us that a future judgment is pending for these fallen angels. In addition, the Word says that somehow the believers will apparently be involved in that judgment of the angels (1 Cor. 6:3).

Thus, in these texts we see that all created beings will face a judgment at the end of this age: all mankind will be judged before the throne of God, believers will have their work judged at the Bema Seat of Christ, and the fallen angels will also be judged for their rebellion. But what is the state of those awaiting judgment during the intervening time?

THE INTERMEDIATE STATE

The "intermediate state" is the term Bible teachers use to refer to the condition of the dead between their death and the resurrection. The primary issues we will consider here are whether or not the intermediate state is a conscious one and whether or not it is probationary. The question of whether or not the intermediate state is probationary deals with whether this period of testing—our present life on the earth—continues after death. Biblically based Christian doctrine has always held that *this* life is probationary; that is, we are tested throughout this lifetime by being given the choice to follow God or to reject Him. However, the afterlife is not probationary; the choice we make here and now counts for eternity. (The question of an intermediate place will be considered in our next lesson.)

Read Luke 16:19–31. This text is one of the most instructive in Scripture regarding the intermediate state, and a wealth of information about the condition of the dead prior to Jesus' death and resurrection is contained herein. We will be focusing on the questions of consciousness and probation.

Who are the main people involved in this story?

Where do the events spoken of take place?

List the evidence given that indicates the people involved are conscious after dying?

In Luke 16, what was the condition of the rich man after death?

What indication is there that the rich man desired alleviation of his condition?

Was there any way for the rich man to change or to alter his condition?

How do these points support the doctrine that the intermediate state is nonprobationary?

In relation to our present questions about the intermediate state, we see that this text clearly teaches that people are conscious of their condition after death and that the intermediate state is nonprobationary. Explain how the following texts show that people are conscious in the afterlife.

Eccl. 12:7

Matt. 17:1–4

Mark 12:18–27

Luke 23:43

2 Cor. 5:6–8

Phil. 1:23

PROBING THE DEPTHS

One group of Christians who differ on the question of consciousness during the intermediate state is the Seventh-Day Adventists. In their doctrine death is seen as an unconscious state in which the person awaits the resurrection. They support this contention by referring to the many times the Bible refers to death as "sleep" (Dan. 12:2; John 11:11; 1 Thess. 4:13 to mention just a few). The Seventh-Day Adventists say that death, for the soul, is actually a state similar to sleep; thus, it is frequently referred to as "soul sleep." But, as we have just studied, there is persuasive biblical evidence that the intermediate state is conscious.

As we saw in our study of Luke 16, there is no evidence for, and there is significant evidence against, the intermediate state being probationary. In the entirety of Scripture there is nothing which indicates a second probation. Dr. John Miley, in discussing this significant silence of Scripture regarding a second probation, says:

> As to any explicit utterance in favor of a second probation, there is a dead silence of the Scriptures. How is this? Probation, with its privileges and responsibilities, very deeply concerns us. No period of our existence is fraught with deeper interest. The Scriptures are replete with such views of our present probation. They constantly press it upon our attention as involving the most solemn responsibilities of the present life and the profoundest interests of the future life. In a future probation there must be a renewal of all that so deeply concerns a present probation; yet there is not an explicit word respecting it. Such silence of the Scriptures is utterly irreconcilable with the reality of such a probation.[2]

On the other hand, the urgency with which the Bible tells us to attend to our salvation gives us further evidence that the choice we make in this lifetime has eternal importance. Look at the following texts and explain how they illustrate this point:

Mark 16:15, 16

Luke 10:2

John 9:4

John 12:35, 36

Acts 17:30, 31

Heb. 2:1–3

Heb. 9:27

THE RESULTS OF THE JUDGMENTS

In this lesson we have seen that the Bible speaks of a final judgment that determines the ultimate fate of the individual. This ultimate destiny is both eternal and irrevocable. That is, the destiny of the individual does not end with annihilation after a period of punishment, nor does the individual have any further opportunity to be reconciled to God after the judgment. In the following texts, what statements indicate an eternal judgment?

Dan. 12:2

Matt. 18:8

Matt. 25:41, 46

Mark 3:29

Mark 9:42–48

2 Thess. 1:9

Heb. 6:2

Jude 7

From these verses we can clearly see that the teaching of Scripture is that the final judgment brings people into their eternal destiny. Whether that destiny is fellowship with God in blessedness or separation from God and damnation, the result is eternal.

The fact that the end is eternal, in and of itself, implies that it is irrevocable. The Bible indicates that sinners are judged forever. In addition to telling us that the judgment does not end, that fact tells us that one's condition does not change. Additionally, the same points we considered in our discussion of the nonprobationary nature of the intermediate state also apply to the eternal state. That is, the urgency with which the Word tells us to come to the Lord, and the absence of any indication that there is a second chance after death both show that the final judgment determines our eternal state irrevocably. Thus, the witness of Scripture and the historic doctrine of the church is that the end of the ungodly is an unescapable, eternal punishment. With that sobering fact before us, let us be mindful of our Lord's admonition, "The harvest truly *is* great, but the laborers are few; therefore pray the Lord of the harvest to send out laborers into His harvest" (Luke 10:2).

 FAITH ALIVE

We have eternal life through the grace of God in Christ Jesus. Let praise and thanksgiving rise in your heart for this great gift, which has saved you from damnation.

Reflect on the Judgment Seat of Christ. How does your understanding of that aspect of judgment affect your behavior?

Take a few moments right now to pray for some unsaved people you know.

1. *Spirit-Filled Life Bible* (Nashville, TN: Thomas Nelson Publishers, 1991), 1460, "Word Wealth: 27:19 judgment seat."

2. Miley, John, *Systematic Theology, Volume II* (Peabody, MA: Hendrickson Publishers, 1989), 435.

Lesson 12/Hell and Heaven

When my sister, Becki, was a little girl, she regularly visited our grandparents in Oakland, California. On one visit, she was with Grandma driving from Lafayette back to Oakland on a bright, sunny afternoon. As they went through the hills that separated the two cities they came to a long, dark tunnel. The tunnel had no lights in it, and it seemed even darker than usual after coming out of the bright sunlight. As they descended into the tunnel, for the tunnel was also on a steep downgrade, the walls seemed to close about them and the only thing visible was the patch of road illuminated by their headlights. Suddenly Becki leaned forward from the backseat and put her arms aroung Grandma's neck. "Grandma!" she exclaimed, "Maybe this goes to hell!"

For a young child, a long, dark tunnel may seem like the way to hell, but as we learned in the previous lesson, it is God's judgment at the end of time that will determine the destiny of every individual. Then each person will spend eternity in heaven or in hell. In this lesson we will study what the Bible has to say about those ultimate destinations, as well as what the Bible says about the past and present places where the dead await the resurrection and judgment.

TERMS USED FOR HELL

We use the term "hell" whenever we speak of a place of punishment after death. However, the Bible uses various words when speaking of the place of punishment, and Scripture indicates that there are at least two distinct places of punishment. Look up the following references and note what word is used for the place of the dead or the place of punishment:

1 Sam. 2:6

Is. 14:14, 15

Is. 38:10

Matt. 11:23

Matt. 18:9

2 Pet. 2:4

Rev. 21:8

✎ WORD WEALTH

Grave, *she'ol.* The grave; the abode of the dead; the netherworld; hell. This noun occurs sixty-five times, its use broad enough to include the visible grave that houses a dead body and the abyss, that unseen world to which the soul departs in death. The meaning of "grave" is seen in Genesis 37:35; 42:38; and 1 Kings 2:6. *She'ol* speaks of the realm of departed souls in such verses as Psalm 9:17; 16:10; 55:15; 139:8; Isaiah 14:9–11; Ezekiel 31:15–17; 32:21. The assumed root of *she'ol* is *sha'al,* "to ask, demand, require." Thus "hell" is a hungry, greedy devourer of humanity, is never full or satisfied, but is always asking for more (see Prov. 27:20). God's promise in Hosea 13:14 is that He will save His people from the power of *she'ol* and that He will actually destroy *she'ol* in the end![1]

In addition to *sheol* the Bible uses several Greek expressions for hell. *Hades* is used in the New Testament in much the same way that *sheol* is used in the Old Testament. It may refer generally to the place of departed souls, but in other instances it seems to apply more specifically to a place of punishment for the unrighteous dead.

The word translated "hell" in Matthew 18:9 is *gehenna*. This Greek word was derived from the Hebrew word for the Valley of the Son of Hinnom. This valley was a place where child sacrifice was practiced prior to the Babylonian Exile. Jeremiah prophesied that this valley would be called the Valley of Slaughter because of the corpses that would be piled up there (Jer. 7:31, 32). Thus, that valley became a figure of the place of punishment—because of the judgment that was prophesied, and because of the constant burning that went on there when it was an area of idolatrous worship.

Second Peter 2:4 uses the Greek word *tartarus* when speaking of the place in which fallen angels are held awaiting judgment. In Greek mythology Tartarus was the place of the wicked dead. The word only occurs once in the New Testament, and, because Peter uses it in reference to fallen angels, some believe that it is a particular place of judgment for the fallen angels. However, some scholars feel that this cannot be considered conclusive based on one usage; it may simply be an alternative contemporary word for "hell" used by Peter in this single instance.

Finally, the eternal place of judgment is the lake of fire. Revelation specifically cites the lake of fire as the final place of judgment for the beast and the false prophet (Rev. 19:20), for Satan (Rev. 20:10), for Death and Hades (Rev. 20:14), and for unbelievers (Rev. 20:15).

A Brief History of Hell

The Bible is clear that hell was not preexistent—it has not "always been." It is apparent that, at some point, hell had to be created as a place of judgment. Furthermore, Revelation 20:14 tells us that hell has an end; it will be cast into the lake of fire. Therefore, since hell has a beginning and an end we can say it has "a history." What do the following verses tell us about hell?

Is. 14:12–15

Is. 5:14; Hab. 2:5

Matt. 25:41

Eph. 4:8–10

Rev. 1:18

We have here a variety of facts about hell: (1) it was made for the Devil—not for humans, (2) it has gotten larger, (3) since Jesus' resurrection He has held the keys to death and hell. These facts must all be considered in determining a history of hell. Another key passage which must be considered is Luke 16:19–31. Some scholars suggest that this passage is a parable, while others believe that Jesus was describing an actual occurrence. In either case there is no question that much conclusive information is given us regarding the place of the dead prior to Jesus death and resurrection.

Read Luke 16:19–31. Where is the beggar taken after death?

Where is the rich man found after death?

From the information given in this passage write a description of the place where these persons await the resurrection and judgment.

From these texts we can begin to put together a history of hell. Hell was created for the Devil and his angels. When man fell, he also became subject to eternal judgment; thus, the wicked went also to hell. At this time (prior to Jesus' death and resurrection) there was one place of the dead; in Hebrew it was called *sheol*. This place was divided into two parts as described in Luke 16: hell or Hades was the place of the wicked dead, and Abraham's bosom was the place of the righteous.

When Jesus died, He "descended into the lower parts of the earth" (Eph. 4:9) and seized the keys to death and hell. While He was there He "preached to the spirits in prison" (1 Pet. 3:19), proclaiming to them that their judgment was just. He also led away the righteous dead to a new location. The righteous no longer share a place with the wicked but are with the Lord (2 Cor. 5:6–8; Phil. 1:23).

Some believe that at this time the place of the wicked dead was enlarged to encompass all of the underworld—this in fulfillment of the scripture which says, "Sheol has enlarged itself" (Is. 5:14). This is a possibility, but it is inconclusive. The wicked dead, to this day, go to hell (or Hades) to await the "resurrection of condemnation" (John 5:29). Finally, at the end of this age "the Son of Man will send out His angels, and they will gather out of His kingdom all things that offend, and those who practice lawlessness, and will cast them into the furnace of fire. There will be wailing and gnashing of teeth. Then the righteous will shine forth as the sun in the kingdom of their Father. He who has ears to hear, let him hear!" (Matt. 13:41–43).

What Is Hell Like?

There are two descriptions of hell in the Bible. One is of a burning fire. Jesus often used the word *Gehenna* to describe hell. Gehenna was the refuse dump outside Jerusalem that was always on fire. Jesus said hell was a place of worms, maggots, fire, and trouble. From that we get the image of a lake of fire and the concept of perpetual burning. The evil ones there are full of remorse and torment (Mark 9:43–48).

Jesus also said that hell would be "outer darkness . . . weeping and gnashing of teeth" (Matt. 8:12). Here the image is one of terrible loneliness: separation from God and man. Those who are consigned to hell will be put into the inky blackness of eternity, with nobody to turn to or talk to—constantly alone. They will suffer the remorse of knowing they had the opportunity to come into heaven with God but turned it down.

The Bible speaks of a lake of fire reserved for the Devil and his angels (Matt. 25:41). Human beings were never intended to go into hell. But the ones who choose to reject God will one day follow Satan right into this eternal torment.

There will be no exit from hell, no way out, no second chance. That is why it is so important in this life to receive the pardon that God extends to all men through the Cross of Jesus Christ (Rev. 20:11–15).[2]

HEAVEN

Once a teacher introduced the topic of heaven by saying, "Most of what we're told about heaven is negative." He went on, tongue-in-cheek, to enumerate the "negatives": no more crying, no more death, no more pain, no more sorrow, no more separation, no more loss, no more war, no more loneliness, and so on! It is true that we are told surprisingly little about heaven and about what role we will fulfill in the hereafter. We are given hints about the great purpose that God has reserved for humankind (Rom. 8:18–23; 1 Cor. 2:9). We now "see in a mirror, dimly" (1 Cor. 13:12), but we know that we will be in eternal fellowship with God and with one another, and the blessedness of that state is beyond our present comprehension.

TERMS FOR HEAVEN

The Bible uses a number of terms and descriptions for heaven. In the following verses note the term or description used of heaven.

Ps. 115:16

Luke 16:22

Luke 23:43

John 14:2

Acts 7:55

2 Cor. 12:2

2 Pet. 3:13

Rev. 21:2

The Hebrews viewed heaven as the dwelling place of God, but, as we saw in our study of *sheol*, they did not see heaven as the place of the righteous dead. In this they were correct for that time. The story of Lazarus and the rich man does teach us that the righteous had an abode in the underworld until after Jesus' death and resurrection. Let us further examine the Hebrew and Greek words for heaven.

FAITH ALIVE

Heaven, *shamayim.* Sky, skies; heaven, heavens. The word *shamayim* is plural in form, because the Hebrews knew the great expanse above the Earth (the heavens) to be immeasurably vast, and its stars to be uncountable (Jer. 33:22). In the heavens, the dwelling place of God is located. However, even such an expanse does not hold God in, for Solomon stated, "Behold, heaven and the heaven of heavens cannot contain You. How much less this temple which I have built!" (2 Chr. 6:18). Since God spoke "from heaven" (Ex. 20:22), and is "in heaven" (Eccl. 5:2), Jews naturally came to say "heaven" as a euphemism for "God." Thus, "the kingdom of heaven" in Matthew is called "the kingdom of God" in other Gospels.[3]

WORD WEALTH

Heaven, *ouranos.* Compare "uranography" and "Uranus." A word, often used in the plural, to denote the sky and the regions above the Earth (Heb. 1:10; 2 Pet. 3:5, 10) and the abode of God (Matt. 5:34; Rom. 1:18), Christ (Luke 24:51; Acts 3:21), angels (Matt. 24:36; Mark 12:25), and resurrected saints (2 Cor. 5:1). By metonymy the word refers to God (Matt. 21:25; Luke 15:18) and to the inhabitants of heaven (Rev. 18:20).[4]

It is interesting to note that both the Hebrew and the Greek words for heaven are regularly used in the plural. The use of the plural could be a way of showing the vastness of the expanse of heaven. It also indicates the use of the word "heaven" as a term referring to another dimension—the spiritual realm.

THE THREE HEAVENS

The most direct statement the Bible makes regarding more than one heaven is in 2 Corinthians 12:2. In this verse Paul says he was caught up into the third heaven; this obviously implies that there are at least two others. The Bible does not specify exactly what these three heavens are, but most scholars agree that they are (1) the realms of the physical heavens (i.e., the sky, upper atmosphere, space), (2) the spiritual realm associated with planet earth—the "heavenlies" where invisible beings struggle in warfare, and (3) the dwelling place of God—the transcendent place of His throne and the eternal dwelling place of the redeemed.

Many references in the Bible use the word "heaven" when they are obviously referring to the sky or outer space—the heaven of the sun, moon, and stars. The references in Genesis 1 that refer to God's creation of the firmament of heaven are speaking of the physical heaven. In Genesis 15:5 God tells Abram, "Look now toward heaven, and count the stars." He is again speaking of the physical heaven. The references are too numerous to list, but a few additional scriptures that relate to the physical heaven are: Deuteronomy 11:11, 2 Samuel 18:9, Psalm 19:6, Isaiah 13:10, Daniel 5:21, Matthew 24:35, Colossians 1:23, and James 5:18.

The second heaven is the spiritual realm associated with earth; it has been called the earth's spiritual atmosphere. It is from this dimension that the principalities and powers that dominate the earth exercise their rulership. Paul probably speaks about this "heaven" more than any other writer in the

Bible, but we do see the concept elsewhere. In the Old Testament, Psalm 89:6 is obviously stating that the Lord is greater than all other spiritual beings, and Isaiah 34:4 speaks of the casting down of the spiritual rulers in the heavenlies. References in the New Testament are even clearer. Mark 13:25 speaks of the powers of heaven being shaken, and Ephesians 3:10 speaks directly of the principalities and powers in heavenly places. The most obvious reference to this spiritual realm is in Ephesians 6:12: "For we do not wrestle against flesh and blood, but against principalities, against powers, against the rulers of the darkness of this age, against spiritual *hosts* of wickedness in the heavenly *places.*"

Finally, the third heaven is the abode of God. It is the place Isaiah saw, where angels surrounded the throne in worship. It is the place to which Paul was transported, where he heard "inexpressible words which it is not lawful for a man to utter" (2 Cor. 12:4). It is the place that John was called up to, where he saw the worship around the throne of God and saw the final triumph of Christ (Rev. 4; 5). And it is the place Jesus said He would go and prepare a place for us (John 14:2, 3).

Read the following scriptures and tell which heaven they speak of. Give reasons for your answer.

1 Kin. 8:30

Ps. 80:14

Ps. 107:26

Is. 14:12

Is. 55:10

Mark 11:30

Luke 3:21

Luke 10:18

Acts 2:5

1 Cor. 8:5

Phil. 2:10

Rev. 6:13

Rev. 11:6

WHAT IS HEAVEN LIKE?

As I said earlier, we are actually given relatively little detail about heaven, except that "it will be worth it all" as E. K. Rusthoi's hymn declares! What does appear clearly in the Word is heaven's utter grandeur—indescribable, yet truly *there* and prepared for us. Write out Isaiah 65:17 and 1 Corinthians 2:9—and then *REJOICE!*

Now, read the following passages and list what they tell us about heaven:

Ps. 11:4

Matt. 22:29, 30

John 14:1–3

Heb. 12:18–24

Rev. 21:1–8

Rev. 21:9–21

Rev. 21:22—22:5

The blessedness of heaven will be beyond comprehension. We will be free from sorrow, pain, and from the limitations of our corruptible, mortal bodies. But there are two questions some have raised regarding our happiness in heaven: 1) How will we be happy in heaven knowing there are people in hell? and 2) since there will be no marriage in heaven, how will we be happy when a relationship, which has been so close and intimate on earth, is sundered?

In heaven we will know and understand far more than we do now (1 Cor. 13:12). One of the things we will understand better is God's justice. Charles Finney recognized justice as being one manifestation of God's love or benevolence. He said, "Justice, being an attribute of benevolence, will prevent the punishment of the finally impenitent from diminishing the happiness of God and of holy beings. They will never delight in misery for its own sake; but they will take pleasure in the administration of justice. So that when the smoke of the torment of the damned comes up in the sight of heaven, they will, as they are represented, shout 'Alleluia! the Lord God Omnipotent reigneth'; 'Just and righteous are thy ways, thou King of saints!' "[5]

In a similar manner, our greater understanding in heaven will bring about a greater degree of relationship, unity, and intimacy with all believers. Because of this we will experience no loss of relationship with our spouses—indeed, our love one for another will be deeper. But that unity and oneness will be shared with the entire body of Christ; thus it cannot properly be said that we are married, but all of our relationships will be deeper. This will be part of the blessedness of heaven: our deepened relationships with one another and with God.

 FAITH ALIVE

How has your understanding of hell been deepened, and how will this impact your witness for Christ?

What have you learned about heaven, and what aspect of heaven is most appealing to you?

Take a moment and thank God for His provision of heaven, and for providing a way by which we can go to heaven.

1. *Spirit-Filled Life Bible* (Nashville, TN: Thomas Nelson Publishers, 1991), 1272, "Word Wealth: 13:14 grave."

2. Ibid., 2002, "Spiritual Answers to Hard Questions: 15. What is hell like?"

3. Ibid., 498, "Word Wealth: 8:23 heaven."

4. Ibid., 1990, "Word Wealth: 21:1 heaven."

5. Finney, Charles, *Finney's Systematic Theology* (Minneapolis, MN: Bethany House Publishers, 1976), 98.

Epilogue

Many times prophetic study can become mired in speculation; in our study we have broadened the scope of the subject and built a more stable foundation upon which to build an understanding of the prophets. This foundation is based on a thorough understanding of the prophetic office and the prophetic message. Vain speculations on sensationalistic subjects produce a kind of "tabloid Christianity." When approaching prophecy, we must always be mindful that "the testimony of Jesus is the spirit of prophecy" (Rev. 19:10). Anytime that the focus shifts away from Him we are beginning to stray away from the ultimate foundation of the subject.

However, the prophetic literature of the Bible does have much to teach us which is vital today. There are many interpretations of end times prophecy, and many people discuss and debate how different aspects of these prophecies are being fulfilled. But the most vital message of the prophets for today is the same message the prophets preached in their own times: love the Lord and love your neighbor. Indeed, Jesus said it was upon these two basic commands that the entire Law and Prophets rested.

The prophets spoke boldly and forcefully about being right with God and turning away from idolatry. This key message is not just an Old Testament echo; the apostle John reiterates clearly, "Little children, keep yourselves from idols" (1 John 5:21). Anything that comes before God, at any time, is an idol, and the consistent call of the prophets is to serve only God.

But even that message is not without its balancing point. True service to God will result in action toward others. James tells us that "pure and undefiled religion before God and the

Father is this: to visit orphans and widows in their trouble, *and* to keep oneself unspotted from the world" (James 1:27). The counterbalance to religious orthodoxy is public service. In the prophets these two messages are married, and they must never be divorced. Doctrinal and religious purity without caring for one's neighbor breeds pharisaical pomposity, which is unpalatable to both God and man. On the other hand, mere social Christianity, which cares for the needs of the body without caring for the greater needs of the soul, will leave people warmed and filled—but lost. If we are to truly carry out God's command to us, we must minister to the body, soul, and spirit; only then have we fulfilled the Law and the Prophets.

However, the prophets did more than just exhort the people to action. Within the writings of the prophets are some of the most comforting passages in Scripture. Not only do we learn that we are to care about God, but we also see His care for us. We see the Lord pictured as a shepherd who feeds His flock and cares for the young and feeble. We see the Lord as a loving parent guiding His child. We see the Lord as a forgiving husband, receiving back and loving His unfaithful wife. And we see the Lord as a servant, who humbly, rather than harshly, cares for our needs.

Another aspect of this comfort is the confidence we gain by seeing God's faithfulness to His Word. In studying prophecy we see that God has *always* been true to His promises. This gives us confidence and hope. And our hope is not just a "wish upon a star" hope; neither is it a blind leap of faith. Our hope is based on the Word of God, which has been shown, time and time again, to be sure, steadfast, and true.

Accordingly, we have a "future and a hope" (Jer. 29:11). We look forward to the Lord's return and to the hope of heaven. Our great expectation is the soon return of the Lord Jesus Christ. Our great desire is to be with Him. And our great hope is to be with Him in heaven forever.